Edited and designed by the
editorial staff of ORTHO Books

Special Consultant:
Alice H. Quiros

Photography:
William Aplin
Martha S. Baker
Clyde Childress
Mike Landis

Illustrations:
Ron Hildebrand

Container and Hanging Gardens

Contents

This book is about nursery shopping

. . . and almost instant gardening

. . . and vegetables, fruits, in containers in the air

What this book is all about...

This book is about plants and people. All kinds of plants and what they do to all kinds of people.

It's about plants in containers—in boxes, bowls, tubs, plastic pails and garbage cans, clay pots and ceramic pots, hanging baskets and hanging bouquets, wire mesh and outdoor carpet, and almost anything that will hold some "soil."

It's about plants that seem to enjoy the confinement of the container—flowers, vegetables, vines, shrubs and trees. It's a trustworthy guide, to the selection of plants, to when and how to plant them, and how to care for them.

It pays special attention to the use of containers in and around apartment houses, townhouses, roof gardens, balconies, and decks.

It recognizes that more and more people who care little about "gardening" as a hobby are enjoying the companionship of plants. Hanging bouquets, shrubs and small trees bring color and the green world into the patio, deck, and balcony.

. . . and bulbs, annuals, and perennials

. . . and hanging bouquets

Containers and plants

Putting a plant in a box, tub, or pot immediately gives
it a new character. The plant changes from a mere bush to
a shrub of distinction. It's like picking a person out of
a crowd of people and placing him on a pedestal.

Many a gardener has found that going down to the
nursery and looking and looking at the most common
plants with an eye to having them around in containers
changed their whole idea of plants. For example, a low
growing juniper is just a ground cover when it's hugging
the ground. But it becomes a piece of art when elevated
in a box, pinched and pruned for a windswept look,
or if the wide spreading juniper were lifted in a hanging
pot and allowed to drape.

Plants seem to have a garden personality and a container personality. As one gardener wrote us: "When you
put a plant in a pot, it's suddenly a prima donna. We put
a windswept pine in a squat, shiny brown glazed pottery
jug and he thinks he is king of the forest. Our plantain
lilies are growing in plain, old ten-inch clay pots, but we've
banked big glass fisherman's floats around the base and
they seem as happy as if they were actually near a pool."

In the Japanese manner

As we gathered photographs for this book we thought we
could see the influence of the Japanese manner of
displaying plants.

Many a container gardener was able to catch the spirit
of nature—in the forest or the high country or the seashore. With a rock or two, some moss, and perhaps a piece
of driftwood, the container captured the spirit of nature.

Years ago, when magazines extolled the small Japanese
garden, we talked with gardening friends about what

. . . and the vertical dimension

It's about unusual container plantings.

. . . on balconies.

. . . around the pool.

. . . or gracing a tree.

they got out of the Japanese garden publicity. Mrs. R. told us: "Our gesture towards the Japanese garden was inspired when we bought a hibachi (one of those little Japanese charcoal stoves). It looked so dinky—rather silly, really—up near the barbecue area. So we framed a small square in the ground just off the patio and paved it. On this we put two lava rocks (we shopped around for mossy ones) and into it we sank a gallon can of mondo grass. The hibachi sits framed as important as you please . . ."

And from Mrs. L: "I planted a cool shaded forest in a large shallow container right outside the kitchen window. I began with a dwarfed pine and a groundcover of miniature mint. I surrounded the pine with a feathery club moss and one dwarf fern."

Looking back and looking at container gardening today, it seems to us that the basis for the contribution made by the Japanese was in the manner in which they regarded plants. Plants were important. Important enough to be seen singly or in natural groupings.

In container gardening, probably the greatest effect for the least amount of time, energy and money, is to arrange a stage for a few choice plants in the part of the garden you use most often.

Pets

As this book was getting underway, we asked a number of confirmed hanging basketeers what cautions, if any, we should tell our readers. Among the answers to our question was this one.

"Don't gloss over the fact that plants in pots and baskets are demanding of time and attention. That's part of their charm. They are my pets. They are dependent on me for their very life. They need daily grooming to look their best and they, the baskets, appreciate watering timed to the daily temperature. They are my pets and should be treated as pets. If you must leave them for a week, hire a plant sitter. The cost shouldn't be more than boarding your pet cats at the local kennel."

Mobility

One aspect of container gardening (and landscaping) has been slighted by many garden writers. One advantage of container planting is in the fact that you can take them with you. An old timer wrote us: "As I look around the place now many a plant in a box or a tub carries me back to other homes and other people. That mugho pine in the little cedar box once graced a balcony of an apartment

It's about plants old, here a 'sago palm'

. . . and plants new, variegated impatiens in a hanging basket

. . . and impatiens of many kinds, in containers and hanging baskets.

house. It was 'loaned' to us to keep until the owners found a proper place for it. Well, I have pinched its candles to keep it small for nine years now, and it looks like it will be around for another nine years. The sago palm in the tub has traveled with us through three 'changes of address.' We bought that dwarf spruce for an indoor Christmas tree about 30 years ago.

"The trees I planted are giving shade in other gardens—tree houses for children of children. I have planted many gardens. These few boxes, cans, and tubs that have traveled with me are the important plants in my garden today."

There's another kind of mobility in container gardening. Containers are portable. They can be moved in to bring in new color almost instantly. There never need be a dull season in the container garden. Even the regular companions look better with the short term visitors.

Companionship
You live closer to plants in containers than with the same plants growing in beds or borders. Especially when the containers are constructed on an apartment balcony, a mobile home terrace or a small patio. You get to know the strange power of plants.

The patio climate, modified for the comfort of humans, is ideal for some plants, difficult for others. Shade from the hot noon-day sun will benefit most plants, but if the morning and afternoon sun are blocked out, your companions will have to be in the shade tolerating group—the impatiens, fiberous begonias, ferns, and the like.

Plants in containers seem to want to be tampered with, to be led into new growth patterns. A clematis that will climb 15 feet or more can be trained as a 3-foot-wide umbrella above a 12-inch pot.

Ivy will follow a curved wire, drape with simple grace, form a formal column.

Watching cucumbers form on a hanging vine is a rare spectator sport. If you don't want a strong vining type in an elevated container, you might try one of the new bush type cucumbers in an 18 to 24-inch box. 'Patio Pik' is a widely available bush type.

When plants are brought close to the eye, the character of the plant becomes important. Some plants are naturally informal, others more polished and formal. Many plants can be trained to change their personalities. Take the geranium, for example. In normal growth it has the pleasant kitchen cottage look, but trained as a standard—a patio tree—it's as prim and formal as can be.

5

This book is about how plants react differently in containers than they do in borders

. . . and plants from the desert in containers from the sea

. . . and how they can landscape a deck, patio, balcony, or roof

. . . and what an old planted tub can do to grace an entry

. . . and how containers can be part of a landscape.

It's about bulbs in containers

. . . and plants that go their own way

. . . and containers as small as a teacup

. . . or raised beds as big as a giant's box.

Plunge into the container world

There's no pleasanter way to plunge into first-time gardening than through container gardening. With the nursery as your partner it's difficult to come up with a failure. If for reasons unknown, a plant dies or seeds fail to germinate, just remember that you did not fail. Just realize that the experiment was not a success.

Whether planting in boxes, tubs or whatever, start with a commercial planting mix (see Page 46). It will give the plants the *aeration* (the air in the soil) they need for root development. *"Aeration"*—don't forget that word. It's one of the most important words in the language of gardening.

Drainage of water through the soil in a container determines the amount of air in the soil. And better drainage must be provided in a container than in soil in the garden. The bottom of the container breaks the blotter (capillary) action of water moving through the soil.

Handling transplants in packs or small pots from nursery to container is a very simple transplanting job. All the green thumbing has been done on the plant before you get it.

Once the seedling or plant is in the container and growing, it will teach you what you need to know about gardening.

Container culture

Do you need a special soil mix?

If you take the word of the most successful commercial growers of plants in containers, the answer is "yes."

If you take the word of the hundreds of thousands of home gardeners who have bought and used a container mix, again the answer is "yes." Garden stores everywhere sell special container mixes under a wide variety of trade names—Redi-Earth, Jiffy Mix, Metro Mix, Super Soil, Pro-Mix, and many others.

The mixes are referred to as "soilless mixes" or "synthetic soils." The word synthetic should not be translated as *artificial*. The ingredients are as natural as Mother Nature could make them.

The basic ingredients for container soils and why.

The organic fraction of the mix may be peat moss, redwood sawdust, shavings, bark of hardwoods, fir bark, pine bark, or a combination of any two.

The mineral fraction may be vermiculite, perlite, pumice, builders sand or granite sand, or a combination of 2 or 3 of them. The most commonly used minerals are: vermiculite, perlite, and fine sand.

VERMICULITE (Terralite) when mined resembles mica. Under heat treatment the mineral flakes expand with air spaces to 20 times their original thickness.

PERLITE (Sponge rock) when mined is a granite-like volcanic material that when crushed and heat treated (1500°-2000°) pops like popcorn and expands to 20 times its original volume.

The mix you buy may be 50% peat moss and 50% vermiculite, or 50% ground bark and 50% fine sand, or other combinations of the organic and mineral components. The ingredients in the mixes vary but the principle behind all mixes is the same: soilless "soil" must provide:

1. **Fast drainage of water through the "soil."**
2. **Air in the "soil" after drainage.**
3. **A reservoir of water in the "soil" after drainage.**

Most important in any container mix is *air in the soil* after drainage. Plant roots require air for growth and respiration.

In a heavy garden soil, the space between soil particles (the pore space) is small. When water is applied to the soil it drives out air by filling the small pore spaces.

In a container mix you have small and large pores (micro pores and macro pores). When the mix is irrigated, water is retained in the micro pores but quickly drains through the macro pores allowing air to follow.

Air space after drainage. Plants vary greatly in aeration requirements or percentage of air space after water from an irrigation has drained away. For example:

VERY HIGH (20% OR MORE) — Azaleas, ferns, epiphytic orchids. Many commercial growers of azaleas grow them in straight, coarse peat moss to get this high aeration.

HIGH (10-20%) — African violet, begonias, daphne, foliage plants, gardenia, gloxinia, heathers, terrestrial orchids, podocarpus, rhododendron, snapdragon.

INTERMEDIATE (5-10%) — Camellias, chrysanthemums, gladioli, hydrangeas, lilies, poinsettia.

LOW (2-5%) — Carnations, conifers, geraniums, ivy, palms, roses, stocks, Strelitzia, grass.

Container soil must have better drainage than garden soil.

Many plants will grow in a garden soil where the rate of infiltration is as low as ½ inch an hour. Under container growing conditions rates of 5 to 10 inches per hour are considered minimum.

Water moves through a column of soil in the garden with continuous capillary action. Break that continuity (blotter action) with a more porous material—gravel or air bubbles—and water will build up where the continuity is broken. A drop of water needs another drop of water behind it to drip out of a pot or into a layer of gravel. The amount of air in the soil after drainage is the important factor in the growth of the plant. The percentage of air in soil is less by volume in a 3-inch pot than in a 6-inch pot. The frequently repeated advice for improving drainage, "add a layer of pea gravel or other porous material to the bottom of the container," sounds logical but actually

---

If you want to make your own container mix

If you are going at container gardening in a big way, with large containers for shrubs and trees, consider the following formulas.

But first consider the advantages of buying the prepared commercial mixes. What are you going to do with the mix?

Few home gardeners have need for large quantities of a mix designed for seedlings and small pots. And, when growing seedlings or growing seed in pots, sterilization of the growing medium is all important.

When the need for container "soil" is limited to a few cubic feet, the purchase of one of the commercial mixes is your best bet.

However, these are the components you would blend together for one yard of very lightweight mix for seedlings and pots:

9 cubic feet of peat moss
9 cubic feet of vermiculite
9 cubic feet of perlite
5 pounds of 5-10-10 fertilizer
5 pounds of ground limestone

For a slightly heavier mix for seedlings and pots:

7 cubic feet of fine sand
14 cubic feet of peat moss
7 cubic feet of perlite
5 pounds of 5-10-10 fertilizer
8 pounds of ground limestone

In all formulas we have substituted a fertilizer mix of 5-10-10 for combinations of super phosphate, calcium or potassium nitrate in the amounts called for in the Cornell Bulletin #43, referred to on page 10. Check the bulletin if you wish to duplicate their procedure in producing the Peat-Lite mixes.

A mix recommended for indoor foliage plants goes like this:

14 cubic feet of peat moss
7 cubic feet of vermiculite
7 cubic feet of perlite
5 pounds of 5-10-10 fertilizer
1 pound of iron sulphate
8 pounds of ground limestone

The proportions for a mix for shrubs and trees:

sawdust or ground bark
9 cubic feet of fine sand
18 cubic feet of ground bark or nitrogen stabilized sawdust

or

9 cubic feet of fine sand
9 cubic feet of peat moss
9 cubic feet of ground bark

add to either of the above:

5 pounds of 5-10-10 fertilizer
7 pounds of ground limestone
1 pound of iron sulphate

you have less soil-air and more water in the container with pea gravel than without it.

Air and water. Take a look at the physical properties of the mixes and the materials that go into them—fast drainage; air after drainage; a reservoir of water. The figures as shown in the chart below indicate percent by volume.

Material	Total Porosity	Water Retention	Air Space After Drainage
Clay loam	59.6	54.9	4.7
Sphagnum peat moss	84.2	58.8	25.4
Fine sand	44.6	38.7	5.9
Redwood sawdust	77.2	49.3	27.9
Perlite, 1/16-3/16"	77.1	47.3	29.8
Vermiculite, 0-3/16"	80.5	53.0	27.5
Fir bark, 0-1/8"	69.5	38.0	31.5
1:1, fine sand: fir bark	54.6	37.4	15.2
1:1, fine sand: peat moss	56.7	47.3	9.4
1:1, perlite, peat moss	74.9	51.3	23.6

Keep it simple

Gardeners who believe that every type of plant requires a special soil mix and like to work out complicated mixes of 5 or 6 ingredients find it difficult to accept the fact that a simple combination of peat moss and vermiculite, or perlite, or fine sand, can be used with almost all types of plants, from cacti to tropicals.

This doesn't mean that the mix you buy shouldn't be tampered with. If the mix is so lightweight that the container will tip over in a slight wind, add sand. Many gardeners add garden top soil to the mix when planting shrubs or trees in containers. When soil is added all the advantage of a sterilized mix is lost. If you are using the soilless mix for growing tomatoes in containers to avoid soil borne tomato diseases, you wouldn't add garden soil.

The standard soilless mixes are free of disease organisms, weed seeds, and insects. All the nutrients needed for initial plant growth are included in the mix. The soilless mixes are ready to use as is, right now. Bring home a

2 cubic foot bag and you have enough "soil" for 20 to 22 gallon sized containers, or 35 to 40 6-inch pots. You'll need 4 cubic feet for a planter box 24" x 36" x 8" deep, like those shown on Page 81.

The light weight of Jiffy Mix and other peat moss—vermiculite mixes is an advantage when it comes to moving containers or growing in containers on roofs or balconies where weight is a problem. Jiffy Mix is less than half the weight of garden soil when both are soaked.

Home-made mixes

If for one reason or another you want to make your own mix—even the mass producers of the mixes are bringing out variations—here's how to go about it.

Choose the ingredients that will give you the blend that fits your planting program. Where the containers receive frequent spring and fall rains, use perlite rather than vermiculite. If your mix is to be used in shrub and tree containers use a combination of ⅓ sand and ⅔ ground bark or peat moss.

The mixing process is the same for all mixes. To make a cubic yard of mix take:

14 cubic feet of peat moss, nitrogen stabilized fir bark or pine bark, and 14 cubic feet of vermiculite or perlite.

or 9 cubic feet of sand and 18 cubic feet of ground bark

or 14 cubic feet of peat moss 7 cubic feet of vermiculite 7 cubic feet of perlite.

Dump the 2 or 3 ingredients in a pile and roughly mix them. Dampen the mix as you go. Dry peat moss is far easier to wet with warm water than with tap water.

Spread these fertilizer elements over the rough mix:
5 pounds of ground limestone
5 pounds of 5-10-10 fertilizer

Note: *Read the label. In addition to nitrogen, fertilizer should contain phosphorus and potash, limestone, calcium, magnesium, sulphur, iron, manganese, and zinc.*

Mix by shoveling (use a scoop shovel) the ingredients into a cone-shaped pile, letting each shovelful dribble down

Store bought soil mixes contain these ingredients . . .

You can make your own soil mix by using one of the formulas in the text and mixing it very thoroughly.

By "very thoroughly" we mean that it must be mixed so each portion, even a 2" potful, has the proper portions of each ingredient.

To mix it well follow these steps:

1. Pour the dampened peat moss and perlite or vermiculite in a rough pile. Sprinkle the fertilizer and lime on top.

2. Shoveling from the first pile, make a cone-shaped pile by pouring each shovelful directly on top so ingredients dribble down the sides.

3. Shovel from the second pile and repeat the cone-shaped pile building and dribbling.

4. Do it again. Make a third cone-shaped pile. It's then ready to use.

the cone. To get a thoroughly mixed product, the cone building should be repeated 3 to 5 times. See illustration.

If the mix is not to be used soon after mixing, store in plastic bags or plastic garbage cans.

To mix smaller quantities reduce the amounts of the ingredients proportionately.

Note: *One cubic yard equals 27 cubic feet or 22 bushels. However, 15 to 20 percent shrinkage occurs in mixing because of loss of air space. For 1 full yard of mix use an additional 4 bushels, or 5 cubic feet. To obtain 1 full yard of mix use 26 bushels or 32 cubic feet.*

Fertilizer — when and how much

When using a mix containing a 5-10-10 fertilizer, feeding normally should begin 3 weeks after planting. If frequent watering is necessary after planting start the feeding program earlier.

Because fertilizers are leached through the mixes when watered, the frequency of watering determines the frequency of fertilizing. Fertilizers will leach from mixtures containing perlite faster than from a mix containing vermiculite. Therefore, plants grown in a peat moss-perlite mix will require more frequent applications of fertilizer.

Some container gardeners prefer to fertilize with a weak nutrient solution, applying it with every other irrigation. When watering plants with a nutrient solution in this manner, a safe concentration would be 1/5 the amount called for on the label for a monthly application. If the label calls for 1 tablespoon to a gallon of water, make the dilution 1 tablespoon to 5 gallons of water.

Plants growing in containers demand closer attention than the same plants growing in a flower border or in a vegetable patch. When you constrict the root zone in a container you must compensate for the smaller root area by both more frequent watering and feedings.

The amount of fertilizer needed at any one time is very small but the need is continuous. The nutrient solution applications, as described above, satisfy the need for a constant supply of nutrients. The use of the time-release fertilizers is another popular method. The timing is taken care of by applying nutrients in a form that becomes available in small amounts as the plant is watered. Check the labels for rate of application. The use of a timed-release fertilizer mixed with the soil is the easiest method to follow.

Garden soils and container soils

Can you convert your *garden* soil into a *container* soil? The organic materials used in the commercial synthetic mixes are almost stabilized in their decomposition. Peat moss, redwood sawdust, fir bark, and pine bark, "*stay put*" in a container mix. We have plants in containers in which a mix of fir bark and sand has held up for five years.

In conditioning a garden soil, gardeners properly add all types of organic material—peat moss, ground bark, manure, leaf mold, and compost, in all stages of decay. All organic materials are beneficial in making heavy soils more friable and sandy soils more retentive of water and nutrients. If the manure and compost add to the fertility of the soil, so much the better. When using such organic amendments or organic mulches of leaves, straw, grass clippings, it's common practice to add the organic matter to the soil every year to replace those that break down.

Materials that shrink or disappear do not belong in a container mix. A garden soil—clay loam or sandy loam—mixed with either peat moss, nitrogen stabilized sawdust, or ground bark, will give you the most satisfactory mix.

Your objective in adding organic matter to get a container mix is to physically change the structure of the soil. And, you can't change it beneficially with a little dab of anything. A little peat moss or a little straw and compressed clay soil makes a good adobe brick. Top a garden soil with a 2-inch layer of ground bark, rototill it into the top 2 inches of soil and you have what a container soil should be—one through which water drains rapidly, with the right amount of air space after irrigation, and with enough water retention for good plant growth.

Use of waste products

In the list of organic ingredients used in the synthetic mixes are products that were once classed as waste products—fir bark, pine bark, redwood sawdust. These are by no means the only waste products that can be used. They are the only ones used in this particular blending of a mix because they have been thoroughly tested for toxicity, pH reaction, and uniformity. Other "wastes" can be used. And more and more waste products will surface as less and less green material is burned or buried. "What comes out of the soil should go back into the soil," say the conservationists. A search for waste products special to your area would be most revealing. Where grapes are pressed there's grape pomace. Where nuts are shelled there are nut shells.

From the gardener's standpoint, it is not true that "what comes out of soil should go back into the soil." Add leaves of walnut or crushed walnut shells and you poison the soil for garden plants. Crushed almond shells are safely used as a soil amendment. Grape pomace when composted has been used as a beneficial soil amendment. Sunflower seed hulls look like a promising waste material, but tests proved them to contain some growth inhibiting properties. Not until pomace can be thoroughly investigated for variability can it be safely recommended. With any organic material, especially agricultural by-products, careful trials must be carried out to insure that they do not contain some toxic element.

More information?

Gardeners who wish to dig deep into the subject of soil mixes for growing plants in containers will find these publications helpful:

Cornell Peat-Lite Mixes for Commercial Plant Growing by James W. Boodley and Raymond Sheldrake, Jr. Information Bulletin 43. Send 25¢ to Cooperative Extension, New York State College of Agriculture, Cornell University, Ithaca, NY 14853.

The U.C. System for Producing Healthy Container-Grown Plants. Manual 23. Send check or money order for $1, made payable to The Regents of the University of California. Agricultural Publications, University of California, Berkeley, CA 94720.

The U.C. manual was published in 1957. There have been changes made in container growing since then, but the principles developed in the book are valid today.

Planting and transplanting

When using the lightweight synthetic mixes, firm the mix, particularly the edges, after filling the container. If the mix is dry, wet it thoroughly. After transplanting, water the plants.

Transplanting procedures, how to shift plants from one type of container to another, how to treat the plants you bring home, is discussed in the following five pages.

When you bring a plant home

When you pick up plants at the nursery, the chances are they will continue to perform as good plants should if you give them the proper care.

Often it's in the first few days of ownership that plants are mishandled. Some of the things that shouldn't happen in han-dling plants fresh from the nursery are:

When you run out of time to plant all of your choices and some plants must be held over for the following weekend, it's easy to let those plants dry out. They may have been watered every day at the nursery.

Don't plant dry plants. Water before removing from nursery containers. A damp (not wet) root ball will not shatter or stick to the edge of the container.

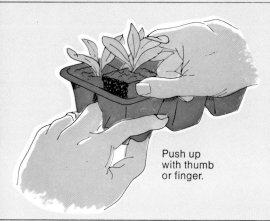

Push up with thumb or finger.

Remove the plant the easy way from cell packs and market packs (2 to 12 plants in a flat). Squeeze the bottom of the container in the cell pack to force the root ball above the lip. In removing plants from mar-ket trays cut the soil in blocks. A putty knife is a good tool to use for cutting soil and removing the root ball.

Don't pull plants out of containers. Plants are grown in plastic, fiber, and metal containers. Straight-sided cans should be cut at the nursery. Plants grown in cans, pots, or tubs with sloping sides can be tapped out of the container. Tap on a ledge with the container upside down. Hold the root ball with plant stem between fingers.

Handle the so-called bio-degradable containers with care. Small size plants may come to you in peat pots, Jiffy-7's, or paper pots. Larger sized shrubs in fiber pots, or balled and burlapped (B&B). Peat pots and Jiffy-7's should be planted below the soil line. With peat pots, punch holes in the bottom and remove the upper exposed edges of the container. The root ball dries out quickly if any part of the peat pot or wrapping remains above the soil surface.

Cut off wrapping that shows above the surface.

11

Root prune when necessary. If roots have formed outside the root ball along the sides and bottom of the container, remove them before setting the plant into the larger container. The pruning will speed up the formation of new roots and the penetration of roots into the soil surrounding

Pot-bound plant

the root ball. If the plant is pot-bound and the roots have formed a solid mass and cannot be loosened by hand, make 4 or 5 cuts from top to bottom with a sharp knife down the side of the root ball and then run your finger through the cuts to fray the roots.

Too high   Too low   Just right

The root-pruned plant should be set in the container soil at the same level it grew in the nursery. Firm the soil around the root ball and water thoroughly. Until the roots spread into the surrounding soil, be sure that the root ball is moist. Because of soil differences root ball may dry out even though the surrounding soil is wet.

Screen over hole

Watering

Before planting in a container, thoroughly water the soil mass. After settling, the soil should be ½ to 1 inch below the rim of the container. There should be enough space between soil and rim of can so that *one* application of water will moisten the root ball and drain through the container. If watering space is too shallow, the watering job becomes complicated. You may have to water and let it drain through and water again.

A mulch of bark chunks, pea gravel, marble chips or a ground cover such as alyssum, ajuga, or vinca over the soil in large container will not only dress up the planting, slow down evaporation, but prevent disturbing the planting soil when watering.

How frequently you should water depends upon the soil mix, the type and size of container, temperatures, wind, sunlight, and humidity.

Bark chunks or pebbles

Soil Mix

Ground cover planting

Soil Mix

9:00 A.M. Wilted plant is watered

12:00 Noon plant has recovered

Many plants advertise the need for water with a wilting that is frightening the first time you see it. With many plants—impatiens, strawberries, tomatoes—the speedy recovery after watering is equally dramatic.

Don't water by the calendar. A plant that needs water everyday during a stretch of warm sunny days can go on an every other day schedule in cloudy weather.

One of the great values of the synthetic soil mixes is that they can't be waterlogged if the container drains properly.

A plant in a porous clay pot will need water more frequently than if it were in a plastic or glazed pot. Some gardeners solve the evaporation problem by placing the pot within a larger pot and insulating the space between the two with peat moss or perlite and layers of charcoal and/or gravel. Be careful not to overwater so insulation becomes soaked.

One way to solve the evaporation problem with small pots is to group them in a wooden box. A box 14 x 24 and 10 inches deep will hold 6 gallon-size containers or the 6-inch pots. Fill with ground bark or peat moss between pots and as a mulch.

Peat moss or perlite

Gravel

Drip irrigation hardware permits many types of container watering systems. Here a length of plastic pipe with a half dozen spaghetti tubes with drip spitters attached delivers water in the minute amount the containers need. It's one way to "vacationize" your garden.

New and old watering devices can make life easier for the container gardener. The Siamese hose connector with double shut-offs allows you to set up a permanent watering system for containers without hose bibb fiddling.

Mist spray nozzles give many container plants the fog they need on dry hot days.

The Shepherd's watering extension makes watering hanging baskets a simple job.

The watering stick, a water breaker, will deliver a high volume of water without disturbing the soil in the container.

Watering a dozen pots at one time was the objective of a gardener who used a length of galvanized roof gutter as the water distributor. Gutter is enclosed at both ends. Holes are punched in the gutter spaced to water each of the pots. It's easier, says this gardener, to fill the gutter two or three times, if necessary, than to water a dozen pots individually.

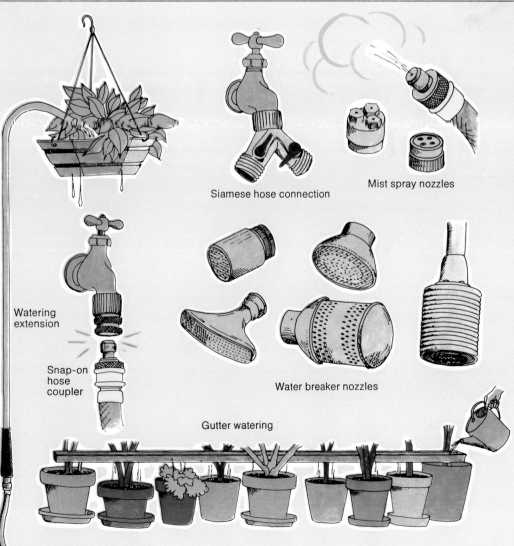

Siamese hose connection

Mist spray nozzles

Watering extension

Snap-on hose coupler

Water breaker nozzles

Gutter watering

Vacationizing

Can your plants get along without you — for a long weekend? for a week? Regardless of your watering systems — automatic, drip, or wick — a plant sitter or at least a visit or two from a friendly neighbor is a necessity if you plan to be away for a week or two. Even the most sophisticated watering systems need attention. You can make the watering job by the plant sitter less a burden in several ways.

Move the containers into one watering spot. Give them protection from the wind and direct sun. The sun loving plants can take filtered shade for a week or two. Grouping plants together forms a mutual protection society, one plant protecting another.

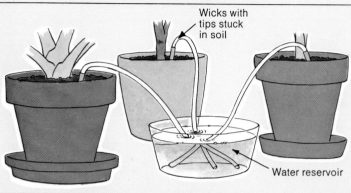

Wicks with tips stuck in soil

Water reservoir

Water level below pot bottom

Soil

Inverted saucer

Wick

Wick watering can be arranged to take care of watering needs for a week or more. Wicks in a pail of water and in the soil of containers will give the containers a continuous supply of water. We use wicks of glass wool and fray the ends that go into the soil. Special wicks are available. A nylon clothesline will serve as a wick.

You can build a two compartment planter box that can be watered and fed with wicks. A metal gutter in the lower compartment holds the water with nutrient solution for wick watering and feeding the plants in the soil in the compartment above.

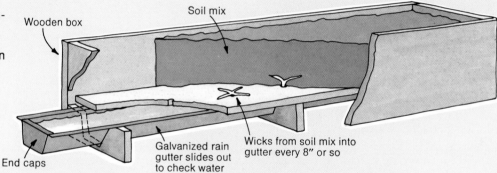

Wooden box

Soil mix

End caps

Galvanized rain gutter slides out to check water

Wicks from soil mix into gutter every 8" or so

Custom-made large pans of sheet metal or home-made wooden boxes made water tight and filled with gravel can act as a water reservoir for a number of wick-watered pots.

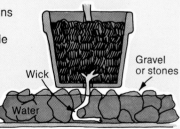

Wick

Gravel or stones

Water

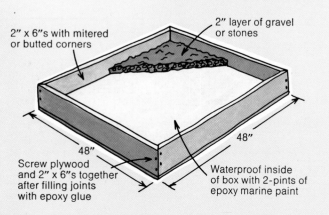

2" x 6"s with mitered or butted corners

2" layer of gravel or stones

48"

48"

Screw plywood and 2" x 6"s together after filling joints with epoxy glue

Waterproof inside of box with 2-pints of epoxy marine paint

Winterizing

Even the most vulnerable plants may be protected from the cold by wrapping the plant and the container in a chicken wire cylinder, filling the cylinder with insulating material (e.g. hay, sawdust, dried leaves, etc.), and keeping it dry with a waterproof cover.

Don't remove this covering too soon in spring— much frost damage occurs when balmy days are followed by cold windy nights.

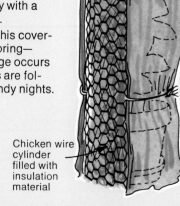

Waterproof cover

Chicken wire cylinder filled with insulation material

Weight

The use of a light weight soil mix — ½ peat moss and ½ perlite or vermiculite — lessens the weight problem. But the weight of the mix when it's dry is far below the weight of a moist mix.

A dolly on casters is a welcome aid to container gardeners with large pots or tubs. For high mobility any large box or tub should have a set of casters attached to its base. The casters not only make the container easier to move but give air space beneath the container. (No hiding place for earwigs and slugs.)

If you are deep into the container business, a handtruck is a most useful

gadget. The handtruck with a trash bag attached lightens the chore of garden clean-up.

Roll rather than lift. To move heavy planters and boxes, too heavy for easy lifting, use rollers of pipe or wood. A set of 3 or 4 wood dowels, 2 or 3 inches in diameter, will do the trick.

Closet clothes poles work very well

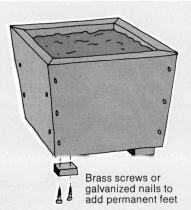

Brass screws or galvanized nails to add permanent feet

Temporary feet can just be slipped underneath

Wooden containers

If the bottom of a wooden container is in direct contact with a moist surface it will rot eventually. All planters, tubs, and boxes should have air space beneath them. If the box or tub you buy or build doesn't have "feet," use small wooden blocks to keep the container an inch or two "above ground."

Wooden containers can be treated inside and at the bottom with a wood preservative containing copper sulfate, such as "Cuprinol" or "Copper Green." Flow it on with brush or spray. Do not use wood preservatives containing pentachlorophenol, such as "Wood Life" or "Penta-treat." Wood treated with pentachlorophenol is, and will remain, toxic to plants. When treating exterior plywood, remember that the edges must be sealed.

Insects in containers

Plants in containers are not immune from insect damage. A good container gardener reminded us of the snail—slug—earwig problem this way: "Container gardens have many advantages, but they also may invite such pests as slugs, snails, earwigs, and sow bugs. The moist atmosphere of the containers offers a haven, like an oasis on the desert, to these moisture-seeking pests. Instead of sprinkling bait on the soil, literally sending out an invitation to any slugs or snails to climb into the pot and have a feast, place some pellets on a piece of fresh, damp lettuce leaf and set it near the pot. Do this in the early evening after wetting the areas surrounding and underneath the containers. The following morning it is easy to pick up your "catch" and dump it into the trash. Repeat the procedure for three consecutive evenings, then again about every ten days until the problem is eliminated.

Snail bait on a damp lettuce leaf

Earwig bait in a rolled newspaper

"Earwig bait should be handled in the same manner. Additional baiting can be effective for earwigs by providing some rolled-up newspaper that holds some bait for any daytime munchers. They normally hide during the daylight hours and the darkness of the rolled up newspapers is an attraction for them."

Since container plants must be watered frequently, they should be inspected frequently, which means that the watchful gardeners will observe the initial insect attack.

A garden grandstand, for almost instant display of color. Rows of petunias, marigolds, ageratum in nursery flats, 4" and 6" pots; with transplants in stained clay pots.

Flower stand built as steps with 2" x 8" risers and 1" x 8" treads.

The almost instant garden

How "almost" should almost instant be? You can set your own pace. The plant suppliers are getting more "instant" every year. There's a shifting rainbow of "instant" color in nursery flats and in 4-inch pots season by season.

Gardeners who enjoy the experience of growing plants from seed to transplants claim that the buyers of plants in flower are missing most of the fun of gardening—all the sights along the way from sprouting seed to flower.

But there are many good reasons for using the nursery as your greenhouse. When you pick up the fibrous begonia in bloom, you have a flower that is 16 weeks from seed. When the nursery is your greenhouse look at the green-thumbing time you save with many of the most useful plants: ageratum, 12 weeks, browallia 12, coleus 10, geranium 16, impatiens 12, lobelia 12, nierembergia 12, petunias, 12-15, snapdragons 14, thunbergia 12-16.

The August wedding

We were forced to prove our good words about instant color when a friend suggested that our home test garden would make a beautiful setting for his daughter's wedding. (It's difficult to say no to flattery.)

So, we decided to do an extravagant job and demonstrate what a gardener can do with the help of his nurseryman—in one weekend plus one day.

Between the strawberry wall and the block of corn we built a flower stairway—a grandstand for a display of potted color. See photograph at left above.

One trip to the nursery, with the thought of the wedding as an excuse for overbuying brought into the garden: flats of white and pink petunias and dwarf 'Nugget' marigolds; a dozen 4-inch pots each of dwarf marigolds, annual dahlias, ageratum, vinca rosea, and white petunias.

The nursery instant color received a variety of treatments. The petunias and marigolds in flats were transplanted into 6-inch and 8-inch pots. The 4-inch pot material went into tubs and planter boxes.

In order to brighten up the garden and find new display areas for containers we found space for two ground level decks in the overgrown shrub and tree border. The best spots were beneath an overgrown Beauty Bush and next to a Purple Leafed Plum. The decks were simple affairs—three 4x4-inch pieces of redwood were laid on the ground to support pre-cut 2x4-inch redwood cross pieces. Only the first and the last 2x4-inch cross piece was nailed to the 4x4-inch foundation.

Instant color in nursery-bought 4" pots is transplanted in planter box for display on deck.

Top right: base of stage are 4"x4"s on ground. Deck is of pre-cut 2" x 4"s, only first and last nailed to base. Decorative bark mulch keeps area weedfree.

In partially shaded area of same garden (right), another stage features cylinders of impatiens.

Our garden is not a full-sun garden. Fortunately, we had the impatiens in large pots and boxes, hanging columns, and hanging baskets, for the shady areas. Where we found a little more sun we featured the fibrous begonias in hanging bouquets.

So there was a lot of color. Anyway, the wedding was beautiful, the impatiens lit up the shady areas, and the petunias and marigolds reflected the sun.

The shade problem

Shade from a wide branching tree, or from a vine covering a pergola, or from the roof of a deck or patio or outdoor living room is a blessing in human comfort on a warm summer day.

In landscaping a small lot for human comfort, with hedges or fences for privacy and wind control, the amount of shaded area increases. As trees grow and increase their spread, more sun is blocked or filtered.

There comes a time in the growth of a garden when "full sun" areas are hard to find. It's then that the gardener starts thinking in terms of shade and plant growth.

The word *shade* never stands alone in the language of gardening. There is partial shade, filtered shade, filtered sun, shadow shade, light shade, half shade, dappled sunlight, deep shade.

Adjoining the patio we have an area that receives an assortment of shade and partial shade. In June it receives the early morning and late afternoon sun for a short period. At all times a reflection from a white wall adds a measur-

able amount of light. The 3 o'clock sun edges into a portion of the planting. Noting growth and flowering of plants in the varying degrees of "partial shade" we concluded that the sensible way to manage a patio shade garden was to grow all the plants in containers. The plants least tolerant of shade could be moved to the spot receiving the most light to increase flowering and set back in the shade when flowering begins.

The number of plants that will flower abundantly in a shady spot is extremely limited but the plants that can be grown in a sunny location and brought into a shade area to continue blooming are many.

The star performers in the shade, in our opinion, are the newer varieties of impatiens. They are excellent pot plants and after blooming all summer outdoors they can be cut back and brought into the house for winter color.

It's well to remember that any words about shade must be judged against the summer climate of your garden. If the percentage of sunshine is low due to cloud cover or fog anything less than full light intensity is risky.

If the sunshine is almost a daily affair and temperatures climb, many a sun plant will welcome some shade.

In addition to shade-tolerant, color producers such as ageratum, browallia, begonias—fibrous and tuberous rooted, forget-me-not, fuchsia, lobelia, and nicotiana, don't overlook the shade plants with leaf color that out-shine many of the flowering plants. Many variegated plants belong in the group. Excellent performers are the fancy-leafed caladium, and coleus.

Quick-change box eliminates transplanting. Can be used for 6" or 1 gallon containers from the nursery. Size and plans, page 28.

Ground bark is used at base of 6" pot to adjust height to one inch below rim of box.

Above shows six one gallon pots of marigolds nestled together. Bark is used as filler around pots and top.

The railing box has plastic pots of daffodils in spring. Later they were replaced with blooming petunias, also in pots made from the bottoms of plastic bottles.

Coleus. The single colored and variegated forms of this plant are available in many sizes, leaf forms and leaf variegations. This year you will probably meet up with the 'Carefree' series. Plants in this series are bushy, dwarf and well branched with small narrow leaves 1-1½ inches long. The 'Carefree' coleus are grown from seed and sold as bedding plants and in pots. They remain bushy in a container outdoors or indoors with a minimum of pinching back. ·

Research with cutting-grown variegated coleus shows that leaf color of a plant changes with changes in temperature and day length. In short days and low temperatures the leaves become narrow and the color is restricted to an area surrounding the midrib. The ideal temperatures for coleus are 70° day temperature, 62° night, with a 16-hour day.

The proud look

You learn to really look at plants as you work with them close up in pots, boxes, and tubs. You deal with plants on more intimate terms, the structure and character of a shrub becomes important.

The personality of a plant can be radically altered by changing the container. Witness, in photographs p. 66, what happened to a mugho pine that had grown old in a box, and to a pot-bound, 15-year-old variegated pieris, page 64.

Container discipline

Not every shrub or tree accepts life in the container with good grace. Generally the shrubs and trees of formal character are the easiest to handle. For example, the classic Sweet Bay *(Laurus nobilis)* and the dwarf forms of the Carolina Cherry Laurel *(Prunus caroliniana)* accept clipping and shearing into all sorts of formal shapes.

Few shrubs have benefited more from the disciplines of container growing than the oleander. Left to its own growth habit it becomes a broad, bulky, multi-stemmed shrub 10 to 14 feet high. When grown naturally it is often used as a thick screen or windbreak.

However, grown as a single trunked tree in a container, it becomes a tailored handsome character. There are many varieties and many colors—single flowers and double flowers ranging in color from white to pink, salmon, and reds. The tree in a container can be shaped to suit with pruning, and pinching out tip growth.

Several varieties are available in nursery-trained tree

Carpenters box holds fifteen square 4" pots of marigolds, moves around with ease, changes when change demands. This one also makes into a mini-greenhouse, (page 29).

Below: scraps of wood pieces nailed layer on layer holds 6" pots of blue ageratum. Smaller version pots of yellow calceolaria.

form. Some of them are: 'Cherry Rips,' 'Sealy Pink,' and 'Sister Agnes.'

For instant color, we picked up three dwarf oleanders in full bloom in gallon cans. Transferred to 12-inch pots in August, they appear, in September, to be ever-blooming pot bouquets. These dwarfs were labeled 'Petite Pink'; and displayed with 'Petite Salmon.' These true dwarfs were new to us. They were developed by the Los Angeles State and County Arboretum and released to wholesale growers for distribution in the South and California. We rate them high as container plants.

The fact that all parts of the plant are poisonous when eaten hasn't dampened the enthusiasm of oleander enthusiasts. Remember that the smoke from burning leaves and prunings can cause severe irritation.

How to keep the youthful look

The life objective of annual plants is to produce seeds. The fading flowers are signals of the beginning of seed production. It is then that much of the energy of the plant is diverted from the production of new stems, leaves and flowers, and channeled into seed formation.

To keep the plant youthful at the business of producing new flowers, remove the fading flowers by pinching or cutting back the fading flowers at ½- to 1-inch *below the old flower head.*

If the seed setting gets ahead of you and the plant has more seed pods than flowers, don't throw it away. Whack it back, fertilize and water it, and watch it start all over again. Plants such as petunias, snapdragons, and verbena respond to this drastic treatment.

Dress up

Don't overlook the opportunity of using ground covers in planters supporting shrubs and trees. For example, wisteria trained as a small tree is a beautiful sight in a large tub or box. A mulch of ground bark is one way to dress up the planting, but for better icing on the cake, why not a ground cover of ajuga for a white wisteria, or evergreen candytuft for the purple wisteria.

Consider the "living mulches" beneath shrubs and trees in containers—Irish moss, Scotch moss, dianthus 'tiny rubies,' thyme, camomile, arabis, and many other hardy groundcovers.

Grow your own pillow packs, sized to fit the need, move in and out many types of containers or locations. See text.

A brick patio with no planting area, finds one as flats of marigolds are set on surface and bordered with brick.

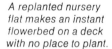

A replanted nursery flat makes an instant flowerbed on a deck with no place to plant.

Pillow packs

Filled with the light weight synthetic soils, any of the many plastic bags that come into the kitchen every day—vegetable bags, refrigerator bags, bread bags, trash bags, are potential pillow packs. We bought tubes of 6-inch and 10-inch plastic, at a plastic supply shop, in order to get a container the length we wanted.

Fill the pillow, bag, tube, or "sausage" with the mix within 2 or 3 inches of the top. Fold plastic at each end and sew, or staple, to close the pillow or tube. Slit plastic where seedlings are to be inserted. To provide watering, insert open-ended small cans (such as frozen fruit juice cans with both ends cut out). Use one or two cans in a small pillow; one can about every 18 inches in a long tube. Provide drainage by punching small holes in the bottom of the container. Start a liquid feeding program after the plants have been in about 3 weeks.

The best way to grow flowers and vegetables in the tubes, or other sheet plastic containers, is to arrange them alongside each other in a nursery flat or shallow box. Only the planted portion of the pillow is exposed to the sun. When plants are in flower, the pillow can be displayed in any fashion—in baskets, on steps, etc.

In containers and in patterned beds the flowers of spring put on their show.

With portable containers, plants that need sun to produce bloom will continue blooming when moved into shade gardens.

Garden bench built on two large flue tiles. Choose plants you love to touch.

The season shopper

The container gardener has converted the business of nursery shopping into a fine art form. In addition to the normal visits to the nursery in the spring planting season, the container gardener is an off season visitor. In any display of shrubs and trees, there are potential treasures for the patio area. But to uncover them and appraise their value calls for more than one visit to the nursery.

For example in early spring, before the spring planting rush is on and the nursery is relatively peaceful, these gardeners look over the star performers of the season with an eye for bringing the season up close. Forsythia, with its swelling buds and burst of yellow bloom, can say "spring is coming" as well as "spring is here."

Many specialties of the South are beautifully adapted to container growing. Take the azaleas, for example. Many of the southern Indica varieties can be used in hanging baskets, others can be trained as standards to become small "patio trees."

The camellia appreciates life in a container on wheels. If rain threatens its blossoms it can be wheeled into the

Deep planter boxes serve as walls of color surrounding this small patio.

21

Bay window boxes give an indoor/outdoor color view to this sitting room. Three nursery redwood planters, large enough to hold 6" pots were mounted on brackets and painted. Moss is used to surround pots and cover tops, providing insulation, moisture retention and "fresh planted" look.

Three seasonal changes have been made to date—bulbs in early spring; lettuce, herbs, pansies late spring; summer planting of garden type chrysanthemums shown in photo.

protection of the porch or eaves of the roof.

With annual pruning, the oakleaf hydrangea (*H. quercifolia*) with its clusters of creamy white flowers in June, and its long, 8-inch, oak-like leaves makes a handsome container plant. It gives a good fall color show with crimson and bronze leaves.

The patio can be the stage for a succession of flower shows celebrating the swing of the season. The plant performers are chosen to speak for the season. Which will typify the garden's awakening at winter's end? Which will carry the colorful banners of spring, the cool green of summer, the red and gold of leaves and berries of autumn?

The mobility of the container allows the gardener to plan special seasonal displays. A "holding ground" in a corner of the garden for containers not on display is almost a necessity when container gardening is in high gear. The holding ground should serve as a plant recovery room for plants, as well as a resting place for containers in their off-season period. The patio is the stage. The star performers can be readied in the "holding ground" (wings) to be called up for their performance on stage.

Our current favorites

Our favorites are many. We have favorites of the season, favorites for hanging bouquets, for containers, for borders and for edging along a walk. This spring we tried the 'Imperial Blue' pansy—an All-American bronze medal winner. Everything the catalogs wrote about it came true. It bloomed from late winter into the summer. It took the hot weather better than any pansy we have grown. The color was a clear light blue with contrasting blueish-violet faces and a gold eye. We used the 'Imperial Blue' in hanging bouquets combined with alyssum 'Tiny Tim' and in wide shallow containers with the golden yellow faceless pansy 'Golden Champion.'

A summer favorite is the Madagascar Periwinkle, sold as vinca rosea. It's the most weather-proof plant we have ever grown. Looks fresh and clean in the hottest weather and stays that way all summer long. As a pot plant it grows to about 10 inches tall and as wide.

Balcony window box, reminiscent of the European style, becomes an almost instant mini-garden when handled like those in photos, opposite page.

Rain gutters, capped on both ends, and attached to fence serve as 4″ pot holders. Gravel used in bottom to level pots, also serves as capillary-action watering device. See page 14.

Left: A fence, with easily attached containers, becomes an ever-changing vertical garden.

Below: Moveable potted plants transform this front porch into a garden where normally "there's no space to garden."

The compulsive gardener

When you look at the ways container gardeners go about the business of finding gardening space where no space existed before, you begin to wonder about the force that drives them. You look upon such things as sections of gutters nailed to a fence to hold flower pots, or melons growing on a shelf on a trellis, or upside down hanging baskets, or living bouquets in the sky, with a questioning eye. Why did they do it? Seemingly, gardening is a force that cannot be turned off. Deprived of normal gardening space, they find space to garden where no space exists. We salute the compulsive gardeners. We understand their plight.

Exterior decorator

A container gardener with plants on wheels is more of an exterior decorator than a gardener. Plants can be arranged and rearranged on the patio easier than rearranging the furniture in the living room. The big difference between the indoor and outdoor living room is that many of the furnishings of the outdoor room are alive.

Plastic container used as portable lily tub. Oxygenating grasses, an aid to clear water, appear under surface.

The instant and portable water garden

A visit with Carol and Bill Uber, the moving spirits of the Van Ness Water Gardens, in Upland, California, changed our minds about growing water plants in containers on terrace balconies, decks, and patios.

We forgot for the moment the "tranquil beauty" of the large water garden, the sound of moving water, and worked with a two-foot round tub.

For our portable tub we used a plastic pool—a 25 gallon affair, 21 inches wide and 19 inches deep. (For sale at the Van Ness Gardens for $10.) This blue container is shown in the photograph above. These containers can be dropped into more decorative half wine barrels, with heavy casters for greater portability. All plants were grown in gallon-size plastic or clay pots and arranged in the tub at varying heights needed for each type of plant.

Hardy water lilies can be planted February through October, in frost-free areas. In winter-cold areas plant in April to August.

The tender, tropical lilies should be set out only after nights get warm and stay warm—May 15 to September 30, depending upon your location.

Winter care

Van Ness Water Gardens advises these methods of winter care: "Hardy lilies may be wintered over safely in the pool if the roots do not freeze. In extremely cold climates cover with boards and give an extra covering of straw. Should it be advisable to lift the lilies before cold weather arrives,

they may be stored in a cool cellar. Be careful that they do not dry out or dry rot will attack them and they will be lost.

"In mild climates they may be left in the pool all winter. We do not guarantee them to live over, but almost without exception they do in the mild winter areas of Southern California. In May get in and see that the bulb is one-half inch under the soil and crown (rough) side up. In cold climates take the bulb out after the lily has gone dormant. Store in a can of moist sand in frost free cellar or garage until May. Plant. Tropicals have so many blooms and are so beautiful they are worth this little extra work."

We like what Bill Heritage says about the hardy lilies in one of our favorite reference books: *The Lotus Book of Water Gardening* (available from Van Ness Water Gardens, 2460 North Euclid Avenue, Upland, CA 91786. $3.25 postpaid.) "The elegant, almost exotic, beauty of water lilies creates the impression that they must surely need much expertise to grow, and coddling to survive the rigours of winter. In fact they require no winter protection whatever throughout Britain and in most parts of North America. Their constitutions, far from being delicate, are robust enough to survive considerable abuse.

"The hardy water lilies are perennial; growth disappears each autumn and is renewed every spring, year after year. They dislike shade, violent currents and cold mains or spring water. All they need to flower abundantly summer after summer is correct planting, a comfortable depth of water for the variety and a place in the sun. The more sun you give them the more flowers they'll give you."

The lily serves a dual purpose; beauty, of course, and its pads act to hold oxygen. Oxygen bubbles appear on underside of pad.

Tub of edible plants (from left to right) are reed-like stems of water chestnut; watercress at front rim; round leaves are lotus; arrow shaped leaves, the Violet Stemmed Taro.

Pool balance

The Ubers have worked out ecosystems for pool gardens, in which plants, fish, and snails live in harmony to keep the pool water clean and free of insects. Four elements are needed:

(1) Oxygenating grasses, most important in replenishing evaporated oxygen. Anacharis (Elodea) is the most used and best for average containers.

(2) Water lilies are essential. Their pads provide surface coverage, preventing loss of oxygen and keeping the water cooler.

(3) Snails for eating algae, fish wastes and decaying matter which encourages algae growth.

(4) Fish for eating such pests as aphids, flies, mosquito larvae, and other insects. (A caution, over-feeding fish with commercial fish food will drastically change the water balance.)

The edibles

We demonstrated plantings of the edible water plants in one tub to show the variety that can be grown. For a measurable harvest each should have a half wine barrel size container.

Bill Uber estimated size of harvest if each type of plant was given a 25 gallon container. "A planting of lotus in April will produce five or six edible roots when harvested during their dormant period in October or November of the second year. The roots of the lotus can be French-fried, like potatoes.

"A tub of 30 to 40 Chinese chestnuts will grow sedge-like, numerous hollow stems to 2 feet or more, from bulbs in the first year. Then, when dormant, you can expect to harvest about a hundred chestnuts. A few from the harvest should be saved for a second year planting.

"An early planting of 5 or 6 Violet Stemmed Taro (*Xanthosoma violacea*) in April will produce arrowhead, 5 to 7 inch, bluish green leaves on violet stems about 2 feet high, then go dormant about 6 months later. Harvest during this dormancy will yield enough tubers for about two dishes of poi. (Only the tubers are edible.)

"Watercress gives an almost instant crop."

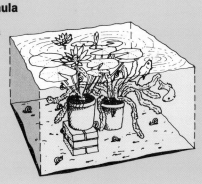

Clean water formula
For each square yard of surface area your water garden should contain:

Oxygenating grass—2 bunches of 6 stems.
Water lily—1 medium to large plant.
Snails—12 rams-horn or trap-door water snails.
Fish—2 four to five inches long.

Looking for a pot to fit a plant – or a plant to fit a pot

These pages were set aside for clear-cut presentation of a shopping guide for plant containers. But after our camera took a look at various container assortments in garden stores; functional plastic waste baskets, buckets and garbage pails at supermarkets; the choice offerings in hardware stores and import shops, we decided that what the camera saw was enough of a guide for a treasure hunt.

Without considering the gadgetry of the hanging basket, there's a big, varied, fascinating collection of containers to choose from. The container you are seeking may be manufactured for nursery plants or an oversize casserole for the kitchen, or whatever. Containers are where you find them. Let your imagination be your guide.

Of course, choosing a plant to fit a container is a favorite pastime of its' own, and you'll find many pages in this book for guidance.

Containers you can make

Here and on the following 6 pages are plans and photographs of a number of home-made and custom built wooden containers.

To many a container gardener, a plan of a box or a tub is more of a challenge than specific directions to follow. A plan is just a way of building something the container gardener can improve upon. That's why there are about as many containers as there are container gardeners.

To simplify the presentation of the plans, we avoided repeating these words about the kinds of woods to use: the woods most widely used are redwood and cedar. They are relatively rot-resistant and weather attractively without paint or stain. The redwood should be heart grade (no sap wood) and air or kiln dried.

Although in each plan, exterior plywood is specified for the bottom of the containers, redwood or cedar boards are equally satisfactory. Edges of the plywood must be sealed, see page 15.

Adequate drainage can be provided with ½″ holes spaced 5″ apart. When using a lightweight, fine soil mix, cover holes with a fine mesh screen such as aluminum fly screen.

Instant color box

This box will hold four or six 1-gallon nursery cans or 6″ plastic pots.

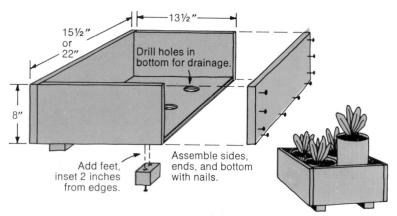

15½″ or 22″

13½″

Drill holes in bottom for drainage.

8″

Add feet, inset 2 inches from edges.

Assemble sides, ends, and bottom with nails.

MATERIALS NEEDED FOR BOX:
Rough redwood—
2 sides: 1″ x 8″ x 15½″ (or 22″)
2 ends: 1″ x 8″ x 13½″
4 feet: 2″ x 2″ x 3″
Exterior plywood—
1 bottom: ½″ x 13½″ x 13½″ (or ½″ x 13½″ x 20″)
Misc.—
Galv. box nails

MATERIALS NEEDED FOR TRAY:
Rough redwood—
2 sides: ½″ x 4″ x 21″
2 ends: ½″ x 4″ x 6″
2 end braces: ½″ x 2″ x 5″
Exterior plywood—
1 bottom: ½″ x 4″ x 16″
Misc.—
Galv. box nails
Waterproof glue

Instant color tray

This tray will hold three or four 4-inch plastic pots.

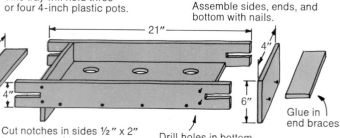

Assemble sides, ends, and bottom with nails.

21″

5″

4″

4″

6″

Glue in end braces.

Cut notches in sides ½″ x 2″ to accept end braces.

Drill holes in bottom for drainage.

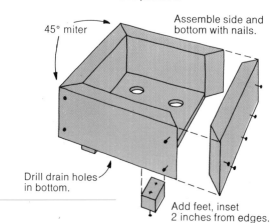

Tailored-simple box

Mitered corners give this box a more tailored look than the box-end planters.

45° miter

Assemble side and bottom with nails.

Drill drain holes in bottom.

Add feet, inset 2 inches from edges.

Add grid of 1″ x 2″ x 15″ sticks and plant Scotch moss to play tic-tac-toe.

MATERIALS NEEDED:
Finished redwood—
4 sides: 2″ x 6″ x 18″
4 feet: 2″ x 2″ x 3″
Exterior plywood—
1 bottom: ½″ x 15″ x 15″
Misc.—
Galv. fin. or box nails

Grandpa Fabri's planter

Saw 4" triangles from sides and drill ½" holes for bolts.

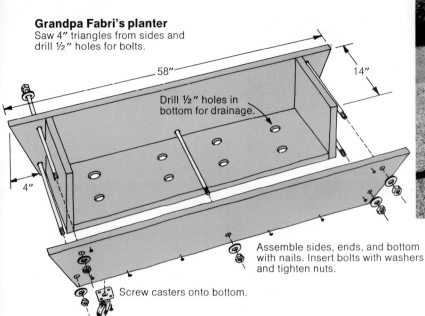

58"

14"

4"

Drill ½" holes in bottom for drainage.

Assemble sides, ends, and bottom with nails. Insert bolts with washers and tighten nuts.

Screw casters onto bottom.

MATERIALS NEEDED:
Rough redwood—
2 sides: 1" x 12" x 58"
2 ends: 1" x 12" x 14"
Exterior plywood—
1 bottom: ¾" x 14" x 48"

Misc.—
5 bolts: ½" x 18" with washers and nuts.
Galvanized box nails
4 heavy-duty casters

Carpenter's tool-box planter

An attractive planter that moves easily from place to place and may be converted into a mini greenhouse.

Drill 1" holes in handle brackets and round tops (optional) with coping or jig saw.

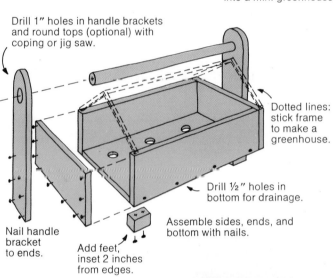

Dotted lines: stick frame to make a greenhouse.

Drill ½" holes in bottom for drainage.

Assemble sides, ends, and bottom with nails.

Nail handle bracket to ends.

Add feet, inset 2 inches from edges.

To make a greenhouse add the stick frame shown on the drawing. Tack 21" sticks to square of clear plastic and lay it over the frame. One side may be flopped over handle to provide ventilation.

MATERIALS NEEDED:
Finished redwood—
2 sides: 1" x 6" x 20"
2 ends: 1" x 6" x 14"
2 handle brackets:
1" x 4" x 17½"
4 feet: 2" x 2" x 3"
Exterior plywood—
1 bottom: ½" x 12½" x 18½"

Misc.—
1 handle: 1" hardwood dowel 24" long
Galvanized box nails
Additional materials needed for seed starting—
4 sticks: ½" x ½" x 10"
2 sticks: ½" x ½" x 21"
1 stick: ½" x ½" x 22"
Clear plastic film: 22" x 22"

Wheel-barrow Planter

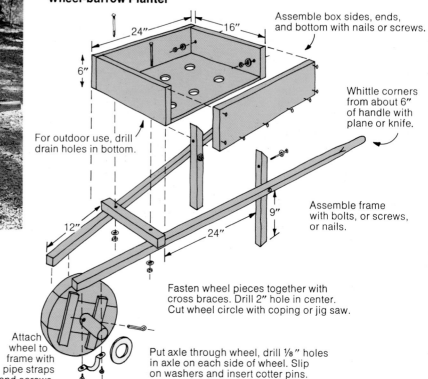

Assemble box sides, ends, and bottom with nails or screws.

24" 16" 6"

Whittle corners from about 6" of handle with plane or knife.

For outdoor use, drill drain holes in bottom.

Assemble frame with bolts, or screws, or nails.

12" 9" 24"

Fasten wheel pieces together with cross braces. Drill 2" hole in center. Cut wheel circle with coping or jig saw.

Attach wheel to frame with pipe straps and screws.

Put axle through wheel, drill 1/8" holes in axle on each side of wheel. Slip on washers and insert cotter pins.

MATERIALS NEEDED:

Rough redwood—
Wheel: 3 pcs. 2"x4"x12"
4 pcs. 1/2"x2"x8"
Box: 2 pcs. 1"x6"x24"
2 pcs. 1"x6"x16"
Frame: 2 pcs. 2"x2"x54"
1 pc. 2"x2"x13"
2 pcs. 2"x2"x17"

Exterior plywood—
1 bottom: 3/4"x16"x22"

Misc.—
Axle: Dowel, 2"x10" or pipe, 2"x10"
2 washers, 2" I.D.
2 large cotter pins
2 pipe straps, 2"
Galv. box nails
Galv. nuts and bolts (optional)
Galv. wood screws (optional)

John Matthias planters

WOOD BASE PLANTER

Nail (or bolt) joist hangers to sides, 20" apart. Attach ends to these hangers.

Paint all metal parts before assembly.

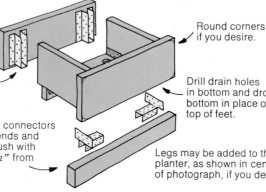

Nail (or bolt) joist hangers to sides, 20" apart. Attach ends to these hangers.

Round corners if you desire.

Drill drain holes in bottom and drop bottom in place on top of feet.

Nail (or bolt) connectors to inside of ends and 2"x4" feet flush with ends and 2 1/2" from sides.

Legs may be added to this planter, as shown in center of photograph, if you desire.

METAL LEGGED PLANTER

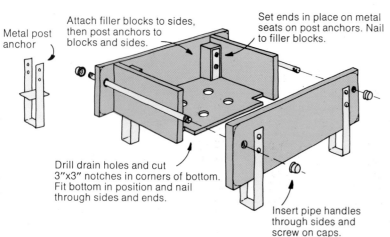

Metal post anchor

Attach filler blocks to sides, then post anchors to blocks and sides.

Set ends in place on metal seats on post anchors. Nail to filler blocks.

Drill drain holes and cut 3"x3" notches in corners of bottom. Fit bottom in position and nail through sides and ends.

Insert pipe handles through sides and screw on caps.

MATERIALS NEEDED:

For Wood Base Planter:
Finished redwood—
2 sides: 2"x12"x28"
2 ends: 2"x12"x20"
2 feet: 2"x4"x23 1/2"

Exterior plywood—
1 bottom: 1/2"x20"x20"

Connectors—
4 joist hangers, 1 5/8"x10 1/2"
4 metal connectors

Misc.—
Metal paint
Galv. box nails
24 bolts, 1/8"x1 1/4" (optional)

For Metal Legged Planter:
Finished redwood—
2 sides: 1"x12"x28"
2 ends: 1"x12"x14"
4 blocks: 3"x3"x9"

Exterior plywood—
1 bottom: 1/2"x14"x24"

Connectors—
4 post anchors, 4"x4"

Misc.—
8 bolts, 3/8"x4 1/2", with nuts and washers
2 pieces of pipe, 1/2"x18"
4 pipe caps, 1/2"
Galv. box nails

Tub planter

This planter is simpler to make than its appearance indicates. You do, however, need a table saw with blade angle adjustment and dado attachments.

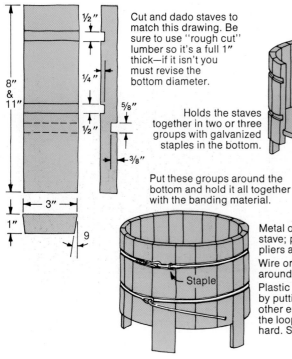

Cut and dado staves to match this drawing. Be sure to use "rough cut" lumber so it's a full 1" thick—if it isn't you must revise the bottom diameter.

Holds the staves together in two or three groups with galvanized staples in the bottom.

Put these groups around the bottom and hold it all together with the banding material.

Drill holes in bottom for drainage.

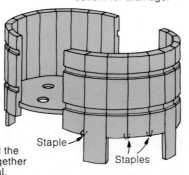

Staple

Staples

Metal or plastic strapping can be tacked to one stave; pulled tight around the others with pliers and tacked again.

Wire or metal clothes line can be wrapped around 2 or 3 times and the ends stapled.

Plastic clothes line can be cinched tight by putting a loop at one end, running the other end around the staves through the loop (see drawing) and pulling back hard. Staple or tack the end.

Staple

MATERIALS NEEDED:
Rough redwood—
15 staves: 1"x3"x8¼"
5 staves: 1"x3"x11"
Exterior plywood—
1 bottom; ½"x18" dia.
Misc.—
Galv. staples
Banding: (see const. notes.)

Scrap or stick planters

STRAIGHT-CUT OCTAGON

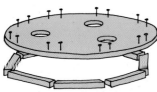

Cut circle for bottom and drill drain holes.
Arrange eight of the 5" pieces in a regular octagon. Lay the bottom on top of them and nail it to them.

Turn the bottom, with its tier of 5" pieces attached, right side up and nail on the second tier. Add the third and successive tiers in the same manner.

If you wish to miter the corners as shown for the hexagon planter, the angle of the cut would be 22.5°.

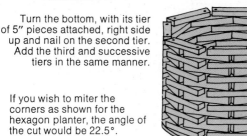

Add casters if you want them.

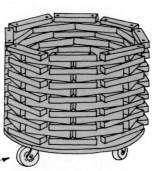

MITERED HEXAGON

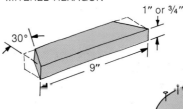

1" or ¾"
30°
9"

The 30° mitered ends let the pieces fit snugly for a more tailored appearance.

As with the octagon, start by laying the first tier on the floor and nailing on the bottom. Turn it over and nail on each successive tier. Add casters if desired.

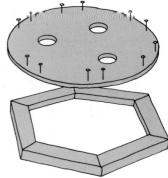

Differences in the appearance of the planters may be had by varying the relationship of the tiers.

Basket

Spiral

Random

MATERIALS NEEDED:

Straight-cut octagon:
Scrap wood—
Sides: 104 pcs. 1"x2"x5"
Bottom: 2 pcs. 1"x8"x15"
  or 1 pc. ½" plywood 15" dia.
Misc.—
Galv. box nails (lots of them)
3 or 4 casters (optional)

Mitered hexagon:
Scrap wood—
Sides: 98 pcs. 1"x2"x9" with 30° miter on each end
Bottom: 2 pcs. 1"x8"x15" or 1 pc. ½" plywood 15" dia.
Misc.—
Galv. box nails
3 or 4 casters (optional)

Wire Cylinder

This planter can be made tall and narrow or short and fat to fit your situation. The dimensions here are just a starting place.

MATERIALS NEEDED:
1 pc. 2"x4" mesh welded fence wire 18"x30"
1 pc. ½" exterior plywood or 1" redwood board 9¼" dia. circle
Galvanized fence staples
Galvanized or copper wire for hanging
Fisherman's swivel
Black plastic film or sphagnum moss

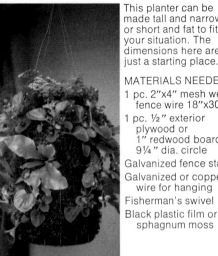

Roll wire into cylinder shape around wooden circle bottom.

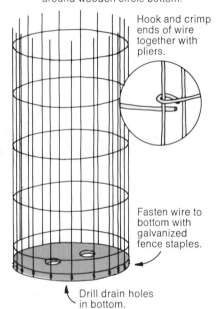

Hook and crimp ends of wire together with pliers.

Fasten wire to bottom with galvanized fence staples.

Drill drain holes in bottom.

Line wire with black plastic film or sphagnum moss and fill with soil mix. Plant through slits in plastic or finger holes in moss. (See page 43)

Vertical Planter

You can make this planter taller by adding 7" to the posts and four additional cross pieces for each increment.

MATERIALS NEEDED:
Finished redwood—
    Corner posts: 4 pcs. 2"x2"x16"
    Cross pieces: 6 pcs. 1"x2"x8"
                        11 pcs. 1"x2"x9½"
Galvanized nails
Black plastic film (lining)

Assemble two sides by nailing three 8" cross pieces between two corner posts. Join the two sides with the 9½" cross pieces as shown.

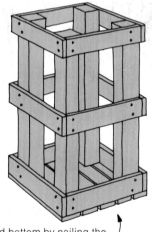

Add bottom by nailing the remaining five 9½" cross pieces across one end.

Line the planter with black plastic film and fill it with light soil mix.

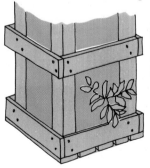

Make slits in the plastc film to insert the plants.

Pagoda Planter

Here's another planter for which a table saw with dado attachments is pretty much a prerequisite—without one you need much patience.

MATERIALS NEEDED:
Finished redwood—
    Sides: 4 pcs. ½"x13"x5"
    Cross pieces: 16 pcs. ⅜"x1"x5"
    Bottom: 1 pc. ¾"x8¼"x8¼"
Galvanized nails
Epoxy glue
Black plastic film (lining)

First saw corners off bottom 1⅝" from corners and dado or notch sides as shown.

1"
⅜"
3⅛"
⅜"   ⅝"

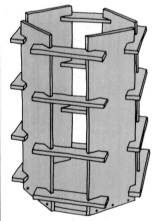

Next nail sides to bottom and glue cross pieces in notches.

Finally, line with black plastic film, fill with soil mix, and plant in slits cut in plastic film.

. . . also an attractive light fixture when lined with parchment. Install an electric lamp assembly for indoor use—a candle will provide romantic light outdoors.

Old-Tire Planter

Draw the star design shown here on the sidewall of the tire with chalk. Twelve points like the hours on a clock.

Cut along the chalk line with a sharp knife. A linoleum knife works well. Don't overrun the corners. You'll need both pieces intact.

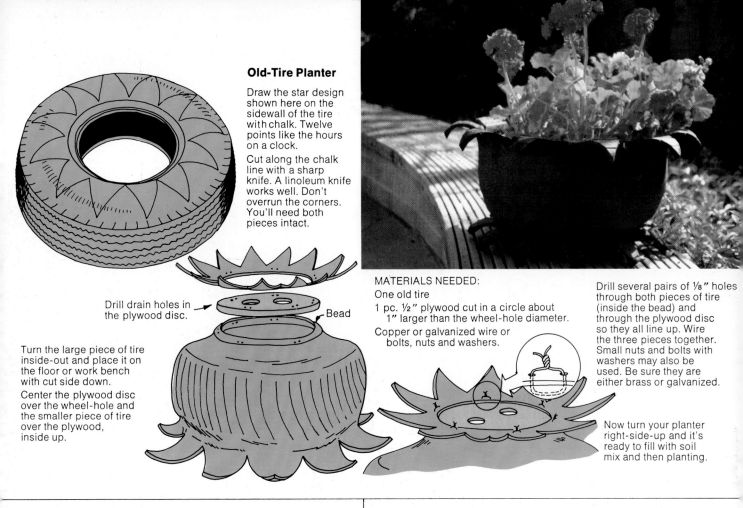

Drill drain holes in the plywood disc.

Bead

Turn the large piece of tire inside-out and place it on the floor or work bench with cut side down.

Center the plywood disc over the wheel-hole and the smaller piece of tire over the plywood, inside up.

MATERIALS NEEDED:
One old tire
1 pc. ½″ plywood cut in a circle about 1″ larger than the wheel-hole diameter.
Copper or galvanized wire or bolts, nuts and washers.

Drill several pairs of ⅛″ holes through both pieces of tire (inside the bead) and through the plywood disc so they all line up. Wire the three pieces together. Small nuts and bolts with washers may also be used. Be sure they are either brass or galvanized.

Now turn your planter right-side-up and it's ready to fill with soil mix and then planting.

Instant Display Deck (10′x10′)

MATERIALS NEEDED:
Rough redwood—
24 pcs. 2″x4″x10′
3 pcs. 4″x4″x10′
or
Finished redwood—
26 pcs. 2″x4″x10′
3 pcs. 4″x4″x10′
Galvanized nails (optional)

Level an area 10 feet square. Lay one 4″x4″ across the center of the area and the other two parallel to it 4′ away.

Lay the 2″x4″s across the 4″x4″s with ¼″ between them. They may be nailed or not as you desire.

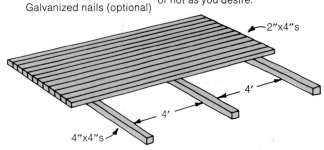

2″x4″s

4′

4′

4″x4″s

Display Pedestals

Assemble two sides by nailing three cross pieces between corner posts, then join the two with remaining cross pieces.

Note: one end is recessed to hide a 9″ pot, the other flush to display sculpture or decorative planter.

Cross piece and end recessed 8″

Add the ends next. The recessed end must have the corners notched to fit around the corner posts.

Finally nail on the sides. Note that two of the sides must be wider to overlap the thicknesses of the others.

... other end flush with sides

The finished pedestal may be painted or covered with wood-grain or marble patterned adhesive vinyl.

MATERIALS NEEDED:
(For 4′ pedestal. For different heights vary corner posts.)
Finished lumber—
Corner posts: 4 pcs. 2″x2″x48″
Cross piece: 12 pcs. 2″x2″x10″
Sheathing, plywood, wallboard etc. (see photo caption)
Ends: 2 pcs. 13¼″x13¼″
Sides: 2 pcs. 48″x13¼″
Sides: 2 pcs. 48″x(see below*)
*13¼″ plus two thicknesses of sheathing to overlap at corners.

The pedestals shown in the photo are sheathed with ½″ translucent CORIAN, an imitation marble used widely for vanity tops. It's beautiful but poses some fabrication problems.
Write E. I. DuPont de Nemours, Wilmington, DE 19898 for descriptive literature and fabrication ideas and methods.

Daffodils of several species and varieties and combined with white and yellow tulips in a colorful entry arrangement that says a warm "welcome" to spring and visitors, too.

Daffodils lend a cheery note to a corner of the veranda. When placed in wicker fernery, a continuous show of color is achieved by replacing bloomed-out pots with fresh blooming plants.

A container with a single flowering plant, popping through a neat ground-cover carpet, can take on the significance of an acre of garden to the grower whose space is limited.

In autumn, think spring

No group of flowers offers a brighter array of color than bulbs; and no picture of spring would be complete without a generous splash of their vivid hues.

Because the container garden is a medium for great versatility, you can provide a display of flowers starting during the bleak winter months and continuing through spring. To do this, you will need to schedule some bulbs for early bloom by using the florists' method of *forcing*. Others should be placed on your follow-up list for blooms that will appear according to their own "built-in" timing.

Growing bulbs in containers is easy. But in autumn, you've got to think "spring!" The first rule is PLAN AHEAD. By the time winter is here, it's too late to turn the trick of *forcing* spring three or four months ahead of schedule.

A big part of the plan is making your selection of both bulbs and containers. (Refer to the Bulb Chart on page 39). Your local nurseryman will be glad to help you with your plan; or you may consult any of the many bulb catalogs for your selection and ordering. Bulbs are often divided into spring and fall types. This doesn't refer to when they bloom but to when they should be planted. If ordering through a catalog, allow more time. Start no later than early summer to make your decision as to types and colors.

After the container grown bulbs have bloomed—forced or not—they should not be saved to grow them in the same way again next season. They should be put out in the ground to regain vigor and develop flowers in future years. Or if your investment has not been too great (and if you can bring yourself to do it) you may throw them out and start with new bulbs for your containers next season.

Your nearest garden center or nursery will be reminding its customers in August-September that spring is just around the corner for the bulb enthusiast, and that's the time to choose your bulbs—not only to get a jump on spring, but to get the best selection. If you're not familiar with names and their colors, or the new introductions, don't be dismayed. Your nurseryman is glad to assist you; and the size of the bulb dictates the size container you will use. Flower colors are usually clearly indicated in the display for each kind and variety.

In making your selections, plan to use only *one* variety in each container, because even in the same species, one color may bloom before another. In a single container, this results in a patchy, unattractive display. Don't be stingy with bulbs. Think of masses of color. If it's many colors you want, grow several containers of many kinds and varieties, each with *one* of a variety, for the most pleasing effects.

These tiny jewels of the bulb world are brought into focus when placed in containers for close-up viewing. Because of their traditional use in rock gardens, a piece of volcanic rock turns a bonsai container, with Crocus chrysanthus 'Snowbunting,' into an artistic mini-rockery. There are many species like the tiny Daffodil 'Angel tears' for very small containers.

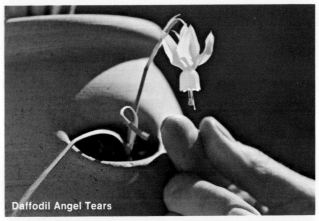

Daffodil Angel Tears

Crocus Chrysanthus Snowbunting

Iris reticulata

Crocus Chrysanthus Advance

The shifting around of different colors when the containers are in bloom can offer a veritable kaleidoscope of spring. As each container's show of color disappears, it may be removed from center stage and replaced with the next colorful performer.

Also while planning, don't forget that you can extend your flowering spring by staggering the plantings. For instance, potting three containers at a time and placing them in storage at two-week intervals. Your spring show should come off on schedule with each succeeding group going on stage as the other takes its bows and retreats from the scene. In groupings, use uneven numbers of containers of a variety for the most eye appeal—three, five, or seven.

If you choose to grow hyacinths, it's better to plant one to a single 4-inch pot instead of planting the bulbs directly into a large container. There's a good reason for this extra step. By blooming time, hyacinths vary considerably in height, color, and time of bloom. When the flowering comes on, you can plant them into the display containers from the 4-inch pots, putting together those plants that go best together at that time.

Don't overlook the miniatures

The little gems of the bulb world, that are customarily recommended for rock garden planting to properly display their charms, are delightful pot subjects.

The dainty and fragrant *Iris reticulata* (see photo above) would be lost if planted routinely in border or bed. Like so many miniatures, they need to be brought closer to the eye.

Check the bulb catalogs for the miniatures of crocus, iris, daffodils and other bulbs.

Visualize pot and bowl display whenever rock garden bulbs are discussed.

It's easy to transfer bulb planting from rock garden to container garden. Witness these descriptions of rock garden crocus by Reginald Farrar in his classic volumes *The English Rock Garden.*

"Crocus imperatis is one of the very loveliest, emitting, first, its prostrate dark leaves, and then, wrapped in twin spathes, a chalice of blossom, opaque creamy buff outside, and feathered richly with lines of dark purple; then, when the rare sun calls, the goblet becomes a wide star of pure soft lavender-purple. Quickly it grows and quickly increases, but because of its loveliness and precocity, it should have a neat carpet to come through, and to keep the tears of winter from splashing its happy morning face.

"Crocus ancyrensis (Golden Bunch) opens in February, a little golden star almost always undefiled with brown, and with scarlet stigmata.

"Crocus susianus (Cloth of Gold) has cups of brilliant orange gold, heavily striped with dark brown varnish outside, and opening into a wide star with so much heartiness that the segments often go too far and turn down the other way. It opens to the first call of the February sun, and belongs to the southerly parts of Russia.

"Crocus chrysanthus can be told from all other golden Crocus by the black spot on the barb of the anthers. The species is most variable but invariably beautiful, the type being of pure stainless yellow, but the forms diverge on to sulphur-yellow and differing shades of blue, with diversities of blue feathering."

Selecting the containers

Your selection of containers will be limited only by the number of bulbs, depth of the pot (always allow at least two inches of potting soil beneath the bulb for good root development), and the fact it must have a drainage hole.

'Scarlet Baby' tulip adds color and whimsy nestled at the foot of a rock wall.

Tulip Gudoshinik

Tulip General Eisenhower

The large and showy blossoms of tulip 'Gudoshinik' and 'General Eisenhower' form the backdrop for small tulip 'Battalinii' in a blue glazed bonsai pot.

You may choose a formal group of containers, or your selection may be as casual as a coconut shell, as classic as a clay pot or you may introduce a note of whimsy, a fish or a chicken (see photos). Bonsai containers lend themselves especially well to setting the stage for your bulbs on display. Bulbs such as *Narcissus 'minimum'*, tiniest of the trumpet daffodils, are real eye-catchers in a glazed bonsai container.

Once you've made your selection—of containers as well as bulbs—you're ready to start. The following pages outline the procedures.

White and yellow daffodils overlook a variety of low-growing container plants that frame an entry path.

How to plant bulbs in containers

First, be sure that each bulb variety is properly labeled before you leave the nursery. A packaged planter mix is sterile and easy to use. Plan to use a light planter mix that won't become compacted. Permeability and drainage are paramount in importance. See pages 8-11.

Refer to the bulb chart (page 39) and before you do anything else, make a tag for each pot; then take out the bulbs—one group at a time— and place them in the empty pot, shoulder to shoulder, allowing only a ¼ to ½ inch separation for soil. Do this carefully with each group of bulbs, being certain not to get them "mixed up".

Now check the bulb chart to verify your choice of pot for height of ultimate flowering, length of time to anticipate before bloom, and normal flowering period (late spring, midspring, etc.) This is the time to schedule your spring-in-winter succession of flowers. A strip of masking tape, which can be removed easily at staging time, should be marked with a waterproof pencil or pen, with date to be planted and stored and the approximate date to expect blooming. Leave the name tags and bulbs in the containers as labeled.

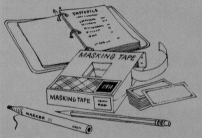

You'll find that simple record keeping will help you. A small notebook and pencil kept in your work area should record each container with name of bulb, date entered cold storage, then later the date removed from cold storage.

Any additional information you may wish to record might be helpful the following year. It's surprising how much detail one can forget from one planting season to the next. These records will help you to set up a good blooming schedule in succeeding years and point up any flaws in your original planning. You'll want to repeat those successes: correct any mistakes.

After this "dry-run" planting, you're ready to proceed. Do your planting, *one container at a time,* following these steps.

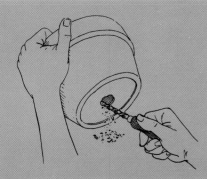

Step 1. Check the container again to be sure the drainage hole is adequate. It's a good practice when using a clay pot or plastic, to enlarge the hole with a drill. (A handrasp or "Stickle-back" drill is handy for this job.)

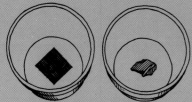

Step 2. Cover drainage hole with window screen or curved pieces from a broken pot. This allows drainage without loss of planter mix.

Step 3. Add bottom layer of planter mix so that when bulbs rest on it, their tops are 1″ below container rim.

Step 4. Which end is up? Don't put the pointed end facing down. The "flat" end is the rooting end. If you happen to plant the bulb upside down, it will right itself, because it knows which end is up; but it will take longer, throwing your show schedule off and wasting the bulb's energy needlessly.

Step 5. Place the bulbs in the pot, shoulder to shoulder, firming them in gently so that they nest into the potting soil (points up).

Step 6. Add more planter mix once you have bulbs in place to cover them. Bulbs are at top of container to allow room for root growth.

Step 7. Water thoroughly by setting container in a pail of water and letting it soak until the surface of the soil feels moist. Allow excess to drain from bottom of container. It is now ready for "cold storage." Repeat this for all containers that you want to go into cold treatment right away.

Step 8. The bulbs that are to follow in subsequent weeks, for staggered planting, should be planted as above but left DRY. Be sure to mark your calendar and don't forget to water as above and put them into the cold treatment on schedule.

Step 9. Place containers where they can get 12 to 14 weeks of "cold" treatment—temperatures between 40-50 degrees. Any spot that's cold and dark is satisfactory. An unheated cellar or vegetable storage unit is ideal.

Storage varies by climate. In moderately cold winters, outdoor storage by covering the container with peat moss or like material in a trench or box is satisfactory. Shredded polystyrene is an excellent mulch. It is lightweight, never freezes and allows water to pass through readily.

In climates of severe winters, containers are stored where they will not freeze.

Where winters are warm and there is not a sufficient cold period of 12

to 14 weeks, hardy bulbs, especially tulips, need refrigeration for 6 weeks before planting in containers.

The purpose of the chilling period in storage is to give the bulbs the environment they need to develop a strong root system and to mobilize their forces for shoot and flower production.

In this storage period, remember that roots require moisture for growth. Soil must not only be moist when containers are placed in storage, but must be kept moist—not wet—throughout the storage treatment.

Up to this point the step-by-step procedure for growing bulbs for display in containers *outdoors* and for "forcing" bulbs for early bloom *indoors* is one and the same.

For indoor display you "force" early bloom by gradually giving the bulbs higher temperatures and light. For outdoor display you turn over flowering schedule to Mother Nature.

Step 10. Now the "forcing." At the end of the 12-15 cold weeks, when the sprouts are 2 to 5 inches high and the roots can be seen at the drainage hole, place the containers in a cool 60° room. After a week or two, they are ready to take the normal

room temperature. They must have adequate light at this point or the growth will be leggy.

After bloom, keep the leaves growing as long as you can. If you plan to put the bulbs out in the garden when true spring arrives, put them in a cool place (50-55°). Never remove the leaves until they are brown and lift as easily as a piece of paper. Food from the leaves is stored in the bulb for next season's growth.

Special note about Anemones and Ranunculus bulbs:

These can be grown successfully in containers; however, they should not be forced. They need no special storage temperatures nor air circulation as do most other bulbs . . . just a rest after their blooming period is over. They must be stored dry, though, or they tend to rot. Under these circumstances, it's not easy to fool them about the seasons. They're tender to frost, so if you want to give them an early start indoors with good light, go ahead. Just don't keep them cold and moist and dark in storage. A spring is not complete without a few tubs of these with their array of colors to brighten any container garden.

Notes for Mild Winter Areas

The showy foliage of the Caladium should never be omitted from the container garden in mild winter areas. These members of the Arum family are tuberous-rooted perennials from tropical America. Classed as "bulbs," they die down in fall and take a winter rest in the manner of bulbs. Grown purely for their spectacular leaf colors, their "flowers" are interesting but insignificant. They should be stored dry in vermiculite or peat moss after the foliage dies back. Bring them out for potting and reviving for the Spring show about January. They enjoy a night temperature that is constant at not less than 60 degrees, with an evenly damp potting mix. Plant about 3 tubers to an 8 inch pot, allowing plenty of depth for roots to develop; but don't over-pot. Use any good planter mix. When the first leaves peek through the soil, increase their light from subdued to north window bright. Keep humidity about 60 per cent. They'll come along much faster if you use a cable beneath the pot—or, if you don't have one, it's easy to use a propagating trick described in this illustration.

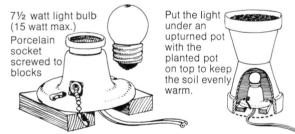

7½ watt light bulb (15 watt max.) Porcelain socket screwed to blocks

Put the light under an upturned pot with the planted pot on top to keep the soil evenly warm.

As the weather warms outdoors on a shady patio, gradually get the plant used to the outdoor location with other shade plants. This lovely foliage adds contrast in color and texture when placed among your ferns and chamaedoreas. Caladiums enjoy frequent but very light feeding (such as light dilution of fish emulsion) and evenly dry—not wet—soil. Be sure drainage is maintained. Try as many colors as you can locate at your local nursery (or order from specialty growers' catalogs)—they include silver, white, pink, red, bronze and green in a riotous variety of psychedelic combinations. (Caladiums are also very good house plants if you provide adequate humidity.)

Bulbs and pests

Bulbs planted in containers are quite pest-free; but an occasional nibble is taken from the flowering parts. The guilty ones are snails, slugs and once in a while, earwigs. Thrips don't tend to invade the container garden—especially with the use of "artificial soils." Snails and slugs are just about the easiest of all the garden pests to control in a container garden if you stay one leap ahead of them.

The foliage of the bulbs is usually unappetizing to the regular pests. If a problem does appear, like with other plants in containers, it's easy for you to take the upper hand in the situation.

Daffodil Delibe

Waterlily Tulip

Blue water and yellow blossoms form a picture with Waterlily tulip and Daffodil 'Delibe'.

In mild-climate areas, the fancy leafed caladium, a tuberous rooted perennial, is an ideal container subject.

At special times of the day, the alabaster white of this hybrid tulip, nestled in this clay chicken pot, catches the sparkle of natural back lighting.

Bulbs for containers

NAME	HGHT.	PLANTING DEPTH	EXPO-SURE* S	PS	FS	PLANTING SEASON	FLOWERING SEASON	COMMENT
FLOWERING ONION (Allium)	9-60"	2-4" depends on size	●			Fall	Depends on species; spring—summer	Many species in a wide range of colors. Long bloom season. Small species like *A. neapolitanum* ideal for containers.
AGAPANTHUS	18-48"	Just below surface	●	●		Spring or fall	Mid-summer	Leave in same container year after year. Divide only infrequently; every 5-6 yrs. Evergreen dwarf forms 'Dwarf White' and 'Peter Pan' (blue) are fine potted.
ANEMONE	6-24"	1-2"	●	●		See Text	Late winter—early spring	See text. Red, pink, blue, rose, or white flowers.
BEGONIA, tuberous	12-20"	Just covered ½"		●	●	Winter	Summer—fall	Flowers in many shades of red, pink, yellow, orange, or white. Becomes leggy in dense shade. Best in filtered shade, cool temperature, high humidity.
CALADIUM	9-30"	Just covered		●	●	Spring	—————	See text. Red, pink, green, and white foliage colors. With proper storage can be left in the same container.
CANNA, dwarf	18-30"	5-6"	●			Mid-spring	Late summer—early fall	Large flowers in many colors. Attractive tropical-looking green or bronze foliage. With proper frost-free storage can be left in same container. Remove faded flowers after bloom. After all blooming, cut stalk at soil level.
CLIVIA	12-36"	Top just above soil		●	●	Fall	Early spring	Yellow, orange, or red flowers. Indoor plant in cold climate areas. If kept moist it can be left in the same container.
CRINUM	24-36"	Neck exposed		●		Spring or fall	Spring—summer	Flowers in shades of white or pink often striped red. Best left undisturbed in container moved into frost-free place.
CROCUS	4-5"	Just covered	●	●		Fall	Depends on species, generally late winter—early spring	See text for variety description. Flowers in shades of blue, purple, gold, and white. In warm areas, refrigerate 4 weeks prior to planting. Withhold water in summer.
DAHLIA	12"-48"	6" fill gradually	●	●		Spring or fall	Summer	See text, page 56. Many flower forms and colors; dwarf varieties best for containers.
FREESIA	10-18"	2" deep	●			Fall	Late winter—early spring	Flowers white, pink, red, lavender, purple, blue, yellow, orange. Fragrant. May need staking. Tender in cold climates. Grow indoors until frost is past.
AMARYLLIS Hippeastrum	24-36"	Half covered	●	●		Available late October	Indoors begins 4 to 6 weeks after planting	Best indoors or frostproof outdoor area. Flowers large, in shades of red, pink, and white.
HYACINTHS	6-12"	5"	●			Fall	Early spring	Refrigerate bulbs for 6 weeks in warm winter areas. Many soft pastel shades. Dutch types are fragrant. Bulb size directly relates to size of flower spike.
DUTCH IRIS	10-24"	Covered 1"	●			Mid-fall	Early spring in mild areas—late spring in cold	Flowers in blue, purple, yellow, orange, and white shades. Plant 5 to a 6" pot. Good for forcing.
IXIA	18-24"	Covered 2"	●			Fall	Late spring	Flowers in red, pink, yellow, orange, and white with dark centers. Tender. See FREESIA.
LILY	18-60"	5-6" fill gradually	●	●		Late fall or early spring	Spring—summer depends on variety	Many flower forms and colors. Plant bulbs as soon as you get them. Require constant moisture but excellent drainage. One bulb to a 6" pot; several to larger container.
DAFFODILS (Narcissus)	5-20"	Covered 2½ times width of bulb	●	●		Early fall	Spring	Plant early and late varieties for extended blooming season. Many single and bicolor shades of red, orange, yellow, and white 'Angel Tears' (photo pg. 35) and 'Hoop Petticoat' are perfect dwarf varieties for small containers.
STAR OF BETHLEHEM (Ornithogalum)	10-14"	4-5"	●	●		Early fall	Mid-spring	White flowers with contrasting green stripe on each petal. (O. Umbellatum)
RANUNCULUS	10-24"	Covered 1"	●			Winter	Late spring—early summer	See text; flowers in shades of red, pink, yellow, orange, and white; best in cool climates.
TIGRIDIA	18-30"	2-4"	●	●		Early spring	Mid to late summer	Large flowers in red, pink, yellow, and white shades with dark speckles.
TULIP	5-30"	2½ times width of bulb —4" to 6"	●	●		In cool fall weather	Early to late spring —depends on variety	Many flower colors and varieties; don't ignore species tulips like *Tulip kaufmanniana* 'The Waterlily tulip,' they are ideal in pots. Require 4-5 week cold period. In warm winter areas, refrigerate 4 weeks prior to planting.

*S = sun; PS = part shade; FS = full shade

Hanging baskets, lined with burlap, decorate Yonge Street Mall in Toronto, Ontario, Canada.

This hanging petunia bouquet, exposed on all sides, requires frequent watering.

Old style lampposts with hanging bouquets are features at Disney World, Orlando, Florida.

One of the more interesting shapes found in hanging wood containers.

Sphagnum moss baskets under eaves, get some protection from sun and wind.

Hanging basket know-how

When a plant goes skyward its container becomes both functionally and aesthetically important. The hanging container must have more protection from the sun and wind than the same container on the ground. When the common clay pot is exposed on all sides to the movement of air, it becomes an efficient evaporative unit. The experienced gardener provides the necessary insulation in various ways.

Wood provides its own insulation and would be used more if it could be shaped in more ways.

Wire, lined with sphagnum moss in both baskets and columnar shapes, give the basket maker the chance to build a living bouquet. The moss has the natural green garden look most gardeners find appealing.

Many materials are being tried out as substitutes for the sphagnum moss — or as insulating material in addition to the moss.

In the illustrations on the following pages, we show the various ways the "bouquet" is assembled and what the inventive gardener is trying out.

As you put together a hanging basket of wire and sphagnum moss, say to yourself "I'm going to be watering this basket 57 or 157 times." Choose any number that will impress on your mind the need to provide *watering space*. Don't fill the container to the very top with soil. The soil should be ½" below the top. The sphagnum moss should be thick and tight around the top inch of the basket. In this way you create a watering basin that, when filled (daily or sometimes twice a day), will thoroughly wet the soil in the container. And wet the soil with one application of water. Watering can be a real headache if you have to add water in small amounts 3 or 4 times in order to get a good soaking.

To keep the basket neat and in full color requires continuous grooming. Remove all spent blooms. Prune off shoots that stray. A few old-fashioned hair pins will come in handy in pinning shoots or vines to the moss. A hanging basket, with its color in the sky, demands attention from the viewer and from the basket tender.

What to do with a basket when frost or age puts an end to its attractiveness? Take it to the compost pile or the work section of the garden and turn the basket upside down. The root ball with a covering of sphagnum will be at your feet. Peel off the layer of sphagnum moss. The moss and the wire are salvage. Clean the moss of any foreign material, soil or plant roots, and use it to build a new basket with fresh soil.

Here's how Mrs. David Bush puts together a hanging bouquet. Tight and full moss lining on top rim. Step 2 below.

Wire baskets, most often used with sphagnum moss lining, come in many shapes and sizes. Half round ones are for attaching to flat surface.

How to line and plant a moss hanging basket:

MATERIALS NEEDED
Wire basket (or wire cylinder)
Sphagnum moss (enough to loosely
 fill the basket to be lined)
Soil mix
4 trays of plants (6 per tray)
Bowl and water (for wetting moss)

1. Put the moss in a bowl of water to soak.

 Squeeze the water from a piece of moss 6 inches square and fold it in half— mossy side out.

 Fit the moss between the top two wires of the basket by squeezing it down. Let it go and its own springiness will hold it in place.

2. Push the first piece of moss tightly against a vertical wire and insert another piece. Pack in more pieces until this space is tightly filled.

3. Repeat steps 1. and 2. all around the basket. You'll then have a neat, tightly packed collar around the basket between the two top wires.

4. Line the inside of the rest of the basket with generous pieces of moss. Overlap each piece sufficiently so that no soil can leak through.

5. When completely lined the basket should have an even layer of moss about 1½" thick. Trim off straggly moss for that neat, professional appearance.

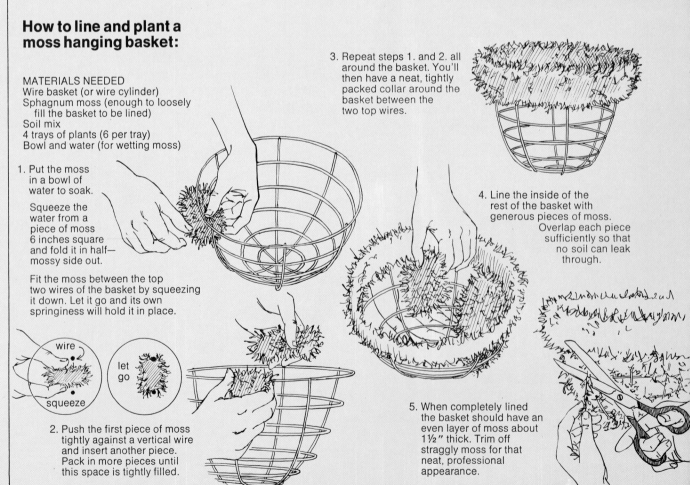

Garden shears may be used for making large planting hole in moss liner. Step 6 below.

Root ball is carefully inserted through moss. Step 7 below.

Here bottom of basket was planted first with idea of righting it and then planting top. Initial planting looked so right, this basketeer left it upside-down.

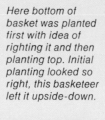

6. Put about 1½″ of moist soil mix in the bottom. Poke your fingers through from both sides at soil level and work a hole large enough to insert a plant—spread the wire if necessary.

soil

moss

crown

7. Insert each plant so its rootball lies on the soil mix surface and the crown of the plant is even with the inside of the moss lining.

8. When the first row of plants is in place, cover them with an inch or two of soil mix and another row of plants. Keep adding soil and plants until you reach the collar of moss at the top.

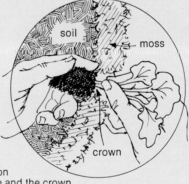

9. Finally, fill all but about an inch of the basket with soil mix and plant the top as you would a flower pot. Use several plants with about the same spacing as on the sides.

Alternate ways of planting —

Here are two other methods of planting in a moss basket. Each method has its advantages and its advocates. Choose the one best for you.

1. Poke holes and push all the plants through the moss where you want them. Then fill the basket with soil mix all at once and plant the top as shown before.

2. Fill the entire basket with soil mix before you plant. Then poke holes through the moss into the soil and insert the plants.

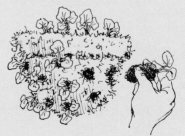

The wire cylinder with wood base worked well for us with a variety of soil-holding liner materials. See page 32 for construction detail.

Above: Cylinder lined with one flat of dichondra planted with dianthus and fibrous begonias. Right: Same basket two months later.

Below: The steps to making a cylinder bouquet lined with indoor/outdoor carpet. Baskets with water-holding liners must have extra drainage holes in wood base.

Planting a plastic "hanging basket":

MATERIALS
NEEDED:
10" plastic pot
Soil mix
7 or 8 plants
Plastic film or
   Sphagnum moss

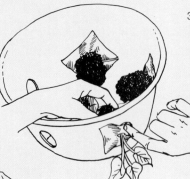

1. Make four or five 1½" dia. holes in the sides of the pot by either drilling and enlarging with a hand-rasp, or burning with a hot metal pipe or soldering iron.

   Be sure there are drain holes in the bottom.

3. Tuck the plastic into the holes as you put the plants through. This will keep the soil from spilling out. Sphagnum moss wrapped around the stem works well, too.

Plastic film

2. Cut a 3-inch square of plastic film as shown.

   Slip the plastic around the stems of your plants.

4. Fill the basket with soil. Mix and add the remaining plants to the top. Water thoroughly.

Both the barber-pole basket, with stripes of Irish moss and Spanish moss ground covers, at left, and the fibrous begonia cylinder at right, were made for us in a garden workshop for the mentally retarded—part of a new horticultural therapy program at Home of Guiding Hands, Lakeside, California.

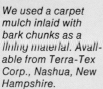

We used a carpet mulch inlaid with bark chunks as a lining material. Available from Terra-Tex Corp., Nashua, New Hampshire.

A new 3-piece "hanging basket"

Here's a hanging basket with unique construction that makes it a "snap" to plant.

The lid

The bottom

The saucer

2. Snap on the lid. Add soil mix to within an inch or so of the rim and plant the remaining plants in the top.

1. Fill the bottom up to the slots with soil mix. Lay your plants on the soil with the stems through the slots.

3. Snap on the saucer and water thoroughly.

Planting in driftwood

Handsomely twisted driftwood or tree branches can make beautiful planting containers.

Decide where you want your planting pocket. A concave curve or the space between two or more branches is the easiest—and probably the best looking, too.

MATERIALS NEEDED

Your piece of driftwood
Chicken wire
Galvanized fence
 staples (staple-gun
 staples rust)
Sphagnum moss
Soil mix

NOTE: If your driftwood is from the ocean you must soak it in fresh water for several days to remove the salt before planting . . .

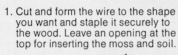

1. Cut and form the wire to the shape you want and staple it securely to the wood. Leave an opening at the top for inserting the moss and soil.

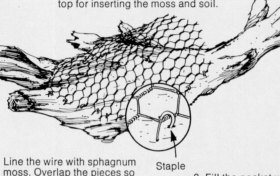

Staple

2. Line the wire with sphagnum moss. Overlap the pieces so the soil cannot leak out.

3. Fill the pocket with soil mix and plant.

Finally add a heavy-duty screw-eye and it's ready to hang beautifully.

Planting in a log round

Rout (hollow out) the center to a depth of an inch or so and drill some drain holes.

Add soil mix and plant.

Alternate: Don't hollow it out. Use chicken wire and sphagnum moss to plant on top (similar to the way its done on the driftwood planter).

moss

staples

soil

Wire tray planting

Old refrigerator or oven shelves, wire mesh fencing, etc. There are two ways:

Bend the edges up so the tray is about 2″ deep. Line with plastic film, punch a few drain holes. Fill with soil mix and plant.

. . . or leave the wire flat, cover with plastic film and punch drain holes. Wire a 2-inch thick roll of sphagnum moss around the edge. Fill with soil mix and plant.

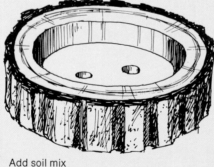

Hanging basket gadgets

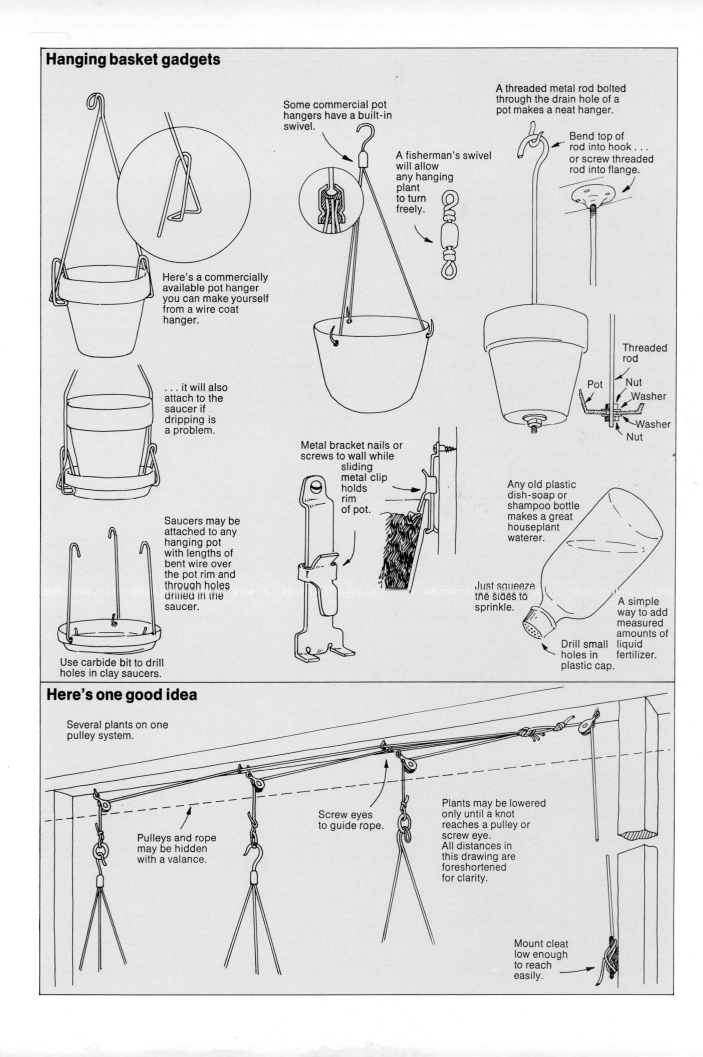

Some commercial pot hangers have a built-in swivel.

A fisherman's swivel will allow any hanging plant to turn freely.

A threaded metal rod bolted through the drain hole of a pot makes a neat hanger.

Bend top of rod into hook . . . or screw threaded rod into flange.

Here's a commercially available pot hanger you can make yourself from a wire coat hanger.

. . . it will also attach to the saucer if dripping is a problem.

Saucers may be attached to any hanging pot with lengths of bent wire over the pot rim and through holes drilled in the saucer.

Use carbide bit to drill holes in clay saucers.

Metal bracket nails or screws to wall while sliding metal clip holds rim of pot.

Threaded rod
Pot
Nut
Washer
Washer
Nut

Any old plastic dish-soap or shampoo bottle makes a great houseplant waterer.

Just squeeze the sides to sprinkle.

Drill small holes in plastic cap.

A simple way to add measured amounts of liquid fertilizer.

Here's one good idea

Several plants on one pulley system.

Pulleys and rope may be hidden with a valance.

Screw eyes to guide rope.

Plants may be lowered only until a knot reaches a pulley or screw eye. All distances in this drawing are foreshortened for clarity.

Mount cleat low enough to reach easily.

Annuals, perennials, vines, shrubs and trees

In the following 22 pages we present a goodly number of plants that perform well in the confines of a container.

To earn a place on our list a plant must qualify on two counts: It must be generally available, and worthy of special attention. Consider our nominations as suggestions. Appraise all plants for their container or hanging basket potential.

In the following chart of annuals, and perennials used as annuals, we have noted the best use of the plant. When the use is "Hanging baskets" the plant can be used alone; plants that are tucked into the basket or column are labeled for "Hanging bouquets."

The common names of alyssum, candytuft, and periwinkle are used rather loosely in many nurseries. There is the annual alyssum listed in the chart and also the perennial *Alyssum saxatile* with the common name 'Basket of Gold.' The common name "candytuft" is used for both the annual and perennial species. The annual is *Iberis amara,* the hyacinth-flowered candytuft; the perennial is *I. sempervirens,* the evergreen candytuft.

The annual vinca, labeled *Vinca rosea,* is not related to the trailing vines, *Vinca major* and *Vinca minor. Vinca rosea* is also called the 'Madagascar periwinkle,' and though a perennial, is more often used as an annual noted for its generous and season-long flowering habit.

Ageratum

Red begonias share pot with alyssum, marigolds, and ivy.

Name	Season-Warm or Cool	Season of Bloom	Form	Color	Exposure* S	PS	FS	Days to Germination	Sowing to flower (weeks)	Comments	Uses
AGERATUM	W	S, F	6-12" mounds	Shades of blue, purple most useful	●	●		8	12	Can be brought indoors in fall for winter bloom.	Hanging bouquet tuck-in. Or plant 3 or 4 in shallow box. Combine with marigolds or pink petunias.
'Blue Blazer'			6"	Deep blue						Compact; flowers profusely.	
'Blue Angel'			6"	Mid-blue						More uniform and compact than above.	
'Blue Mink'			12"	Light blue						More vigorous than above. Large flower heads.	
'Royal Blazer'			6"	Purple						Dwarf as 'Blue Blazer' but later blooming.	
'Summer Snow'			6"	White						Similar plant form as 'Blue Blazer.'	
ALYSSUM	W	Sp, S, F	3-8" low trailing mat; 10-15" spread	White, purple, rose	●			8	8	Fast growing, tough plants. Profuse bloomer. Faintly fragrant.	Low growing. 'Tiny Tim' most useful in hanging bouquets. A most versatile plant. Use as ground cover in tubbed shrub or tree.
'Carpet of Snow'			4"	White						Forms very dense carpet of flowers.	
'Tiny Tim'			2-3"	White						Early flowering miniature.	
AAS 'Rosie O'Day'			4"	Deep rose						Retains deep color well.	
AAS 'Royal Carpet'			3-5"	Violet-purple						Very tough; profuse flowers.	
'Oriental Night'			4"	Dark purple						Compact plants similar to 'Tiny Tim.'	

*S=sun; PS=part shade; FS=full shade

Alyssum 'Rosie O'Day' and pansies

White alyssum and dwarf marigolds

Name	Season-Warm or Cool	Season-of Bloom	Form	Color	Exposure* S	PS	FS	Days to Germination	Sowing to flower (weeks)	Comments	Uses
BACHELOR BUTTON	W	Sp, S	10-36″ erect, bushy	Blue, red, pink, white shades	●	●		10	10	Scorched early by summer heat.	Dwarf forms best for pots. Favored as cut flowers and old-time boutonnieres.
'Jubilee Gem'			12″	Deep blue						Neat bushy habit. Good blue color.	
'Polka Dot Mix'			15″	Blue, red, pink, white						Good habit. Silvery foliage with ruffled flowers.	
AAS 'Snowball'			12″	White						Heat and disease resistant. Long bloom period.	
BALSAM	W	S, F	8-30″ erect	Wide range pink to purple, orange shades, scarlet & white		●		8	12	Takes full sun in cool areas; Camellia and Bush types best for containers.	Hanging bouquets combine with the earliest-to-bloom annuals.
'Tom Thumb'			10″	Color mix						Very compact habit. Holds double flowers above foliage. Profuse bloomer.	
BEGONIA, fibrous	C-W	S, F	6-14″ erect, bushy	Red, rose, pink shades and white	●	●	●	14-21	16	Green foliage varieties will develop bronze color in full sun. Summer sow—winter bloom. See Begonia variety chart.	Hanging bouquets. Hanging columns. Our favorite combination: 'Viva' and 'Scarletta' for a red and white living bouquet.
BROWALLIA	W	S, F	8-18″ spreading	Blue shades, white		●		15	12	Sow in summer for winter bloom. In cold areas can be brought indoors. Blooms profusely.	Hanging baskets. One of the few brilliant blue flowers. Excellent cut flower. In fall cut back and pot up for winter bloom indoors.
'Blue Bells Improved'			8-10″	Lavender-blue						Base-branching, needs no pinching. Neat and compact habit.	
'Silver Bells'			8-10″	White						Same fine habit as above.	
'Sky Bells'			8-10″	Powder blue						Good habit. Large flowers.	

*S＝sun; PS＝part shade; FS＝full shade

Celosia plumosa, dwarf, mixed.

White candytuft with English daisies and blue ageratum.

Coleus

Name	Season-Warm or Cool	Season of Bloom	Form	Color	Exposure* S	Exposure* PS	Exposure* FS	Days to Germination	Sowing to flower (weeks)	Comments	Uses
CALENDULA	C-W	Sp, S	6-24" compact, spreading	Orange, yellow shades, white	●	●		10	8	Best in cool temperatures. Winter bloom from summer sowing. Earliest color in winter and spring from fall transplanting.	Plant for late winter color in pots, boxes, tubs. Will take sharp frosts.
'Pacific Beauty'			18"	Many shades of above colors						Heat resistant. Long stemmed flowers great for cutting.	
CANDYTUFT (Annual Iberis)	C-W	Sp, S	6-15" mounds	Red, pink, lavender, purple shades, and white	●	●		8	10	Best in cool summer areas. Hyacinth flowering types less hardy, not as good in pots. Sow 2-3 weeks apart for continuous bloom. Mild winter bloom from summer sowing.	Pots, window boxes. Dwarf hybrids best in hanging bouquets. Good cut flower.
'Umbellata Dwarf Fairy'			8"	Many shades of above						Very compact plants. Somewhat heat resistant.	
CELOSIA	W	S, F	6-36" erect	Yellow, gold, purple, pink, red shades, white	●			10	8	Dwarf varieties best for containers. Many bright colored varieties available. Cold sensitive.	We planted the plumes in a box next to the carrots.
PLUMOSA TYPE 'Fairy Fountains'			14"	Color mix						Good base branching habit. Vigorous grower with long bloom.	
'Fiery Feather'			12"	Red						Uniform pyramid shaped plumes.	
COCKSCOMB TYPE 'Jewel Box'			4-8"	Color mix						Compact miniature plants covered with large combs.	
COLEUS	W		12-30" erect	Wide variety of foliage color combinations in red, pink, green, yellow, and rose		●		10		8-10 weeks from sowing to mature size. Direct filtered light best indoors. Pinch tips to encourage branching. Many different leaf forms.	Grown for spectacular leaf color. Pot for light shade outdoors, indirect light indoors.
'Carefree'			12"	Available as mix or separate colors.		●				Self-branching. Needs no pinching to maintain excellent habit. Small closely spaced leaves.	
'Rainbow'			15"	Available as mix or separate colors.						More vigorous and larger leaves than above, needs pinching. Fringed or finely serrated leaves.	
'Magic Lace'			18"	Mixed colors						Needs pinching. Deeply cut, ruffled leaves.	

*S = sun; PS = part shade; FS = full shade

Dianthus in tub with Irish moss.

Gazania

Geranium 'sprinter'

Name	Season-Warm or Cool	Season of Bloom	Form	Color	Exposure* S	PS	FS	Days to Germination	Sowing to flower (weeks)	Comments	Uses
DIANTHUS	W	Sp, S, F	3-15″ erect, bushy	White, pink, salmon, red rose, violet	●	●		7	6-12	Lacy blue-grey foliage. Afternoon shade in hot areas. Fragrant flowers.	Dwarf varieties best in pots. We used 'Wee Willie' in early season hanging bouquet combined with strawberries.
'Baby Doll'			8″	Vivid shades of red, pink, violet and white					6-8	Sturdy and compact plant. Plain edged, single flowers.	
AAS 'China Doll'			10-12″	Pink, red, and salmon shades edged white					10-12	Compact, base-branching. Double flowers in clusters.	
AAS 'Magic Charms'			6″	White, rose scarlet, pink shades					6-8	Excellent base-branching; compact habit. Fringed, single blossoms, some speckled.	
AAS 'Queen of Hearts'			15″	Brilliant scarlet-red					12-15	Compact, base-branching; vigorous habit. Single flowers.	
'Wee Willie'			3″ compact mound	Red, rose, shades and white				7	6-8	Long blooming, sweet scented, single flowers. Very compact plants.	
GAZANIA 'Sunshine Mix'	W	S, F	8″ erect	Cream, yellow, orange, pink, bronze, red, some with contrasting zones	●			10	10	Daisy-like flowers, long blooming. Thrives in hot dry areas. Large brightly colored 5″ flowers, many with contrasting centers.	Colorful in large pots and boxes. Blooms until frost.
GERANIUM (From Seed)	W	S, F	18-24″ erect	Red, scarlet, pink, rose, pink shades, salmon	●			14-21	16		A favorite of long standing for containers indoors and outdoors.
'Carefree'			24″ erect with basal branching	Separate colors or mix						See text (page 57).	
'Sprinter'			18″ erect							Dwarfer than 'Carefree' and slightly earlier flowering.	
IMPATIENS	W	S, F	10-20″ mounds	Solid and bi-colored shades of red, pink, violet, orange and white		●		18	12	Indoor or outdoor winter bloom from summer sowing. Blooms profusely. See Impatiens chart for varieties.	In pots, tubs, hanging baskets or hanging bouquets. Solves problem of color in the shade.

*S = sun; PS = part shade; FS = full shade

Lobelia with white alyssum, red fibrous begonias

Pink petunias, yellow nasturtium, blue lobelia, blue pansies

Centerpiece of pansies

Name	Season—Warm or Cool	Season of Bloom	Form	Color	Exposure* S	PS	FS	Days to Germination	Sowing to flower (weeks)	Comments	Uses
LOBELIA	W	S, F	5-8" trailing or erect	Lavender-blue, pink, white	●	●		18	12	Shearing after first flowering may provide second bloom. Slow from seed. Blooms profusely.	Trailing types in hanging baskets or at base of shrubs in boxes. Compact types in pots and boxes. Combine with alyssum, marigolds.
'Crystal Palace'			5" erect	Dark blue						Dark bronze-green foliage.	
'Heavenly'			8" erect	Midblue						Flowers are twice the size of other lobelias.	
'Blue Cascade'			8" trailing	Light blue						Green foliage. Large flowers.	
'Sapphire'			8" trailing	Dark blue, white centers						Light green foliage.	
MARIGOLDS	W	S, F	6-36" erect, or bushy	Yellow, gold, red, orange shades, solid and bicolors	●			7	8-10	Sizes available for every container. See Marigold chart for varieties. Easy care. Profuse bloomer.	Dwarf varieties in hanging bouquets. Taller varieties as cut flowers.
NASTURTIUM	C-W	Sp, S, F	12-15" bushy or 24" trailing vine	Maroon, red, orange, rose, yellow, cream, single and bicolors	●			10	6	Best for cool climates. Leaves, seeds, and flowers edible. Profuse bloomers. Prefer dry soil.	Quick color in pots and hanging baskets. Good cut flowers.
'Dwarf Double Jewel'			12" bushy	Rose, mahogany, yellow, orange-scarlet						Compact habit. Double flowers held above foliage.	
AAS 'Double Gleam'			24" trailing	Complete nasturtium range						Large, sweet scented flowers, double and semi-double.	
NEMESIA	C	Sp, S	8-24" erect	All colors but green	●			10	12	Lacks heat tolerance. 'Nana Compacta' (10") dwarf varieties are best for containers.	Charming in hanging bouquet, in pots and window boxes. Pinch to make bushy.
'Carnival Blend'			10"	White, red, orange, and yellow						Compact, base-branching plant.	
NICOTIANA	W	S, F	8-36" erect or bushy	Red, rose, lavender, green shades and white	●	●		15	8-10	Afternoon shade in hot areas. Fragrant. Most flowers open early morning and at dusk.	Excellent in pots. Cut flowers.
'White Bedder'			15" bushy	White						Profuse bloom. Compact, sturdy plants.	
'Crimson Bladder'			18" bushy	Crimson						Same as above.	

*S=sun; PS=part shade; FS=full shade

52

Petunias in hanging cylinder

Dwarf nasturtium

Name	Season- Warm or Cool	Season of Bloom	Form	Color	Exposure* S	PS	FS	Days to Germination	Sowing to flower (weeks)	Comments	Uses
NIEREMBERGIA	W	S, F	6-10" mat	Violet-blue	●	●		15	16	Compact, densely branched. slightly spreading plant. Perennial in mild winter areas. Profuse bloom.	Pots and hanging baskets.
'Purple Robe'			6"	Violet-blue						Forms dense mat covered with flowers.	
PANSY	C	Sp, S, F	6-8" erect	Full range, some blotched	●	●		10		In mild areas winter bloom from summer sowing. Primarily spring bloom in hot summer areas. All varieties suited for containers.	Hanging bouquets in mixed colors. Many uses in pots, window boxes and planters.
AAS 'Imperial Blue'			7"	Light blue with violet face, gold eye						Heat resistant. Long bloom. Large flowers.	
AAS 'Majestic Giants'			6"	Wide range, blotched						Large 4" flowers. Blooms through summer.	
PETUNIAS	W	Sp, S, F	12-15" bushy mounds	Wide range, red, pink, blue, purple, yellow, orange, white, single and bicolored shades	●			12	12-15	Very versatile. All do well in containers. F-1 hybrids best performers. Choose variety for color and flower form, single or double, ruffled or plain edged.	Versatile. All uses: containers, hanging baskets and hanging bouquets.
Grandiflora varieties										Greatest vigor. Ruffled large flowers but not as prolific flowering as Multifloras.	
Multiflora varieties										More compact and uniform than Grandifloras. Best weather resistance. Smaller flowers than above but greater total bloom. Plain-edged flowers.	
PHLOX, annual	C-W	S, F	6-15" erect or bushy	Blue, violet, crimson, pink, yellow, white, shades	●			12	10	Some varieties are heat sensitive. Transplanting difficult. Small seedlings often flower best.	Grow in pots and hanging bouquets. Fine cut flowers.
'Dwarf Beauty Mix'			6-7"							Heat resistant, compact plant. Profuse bloom.	
'Globe Mix'			8"							Base-branching, ball shaped plants. Heat resistant. Large flowers.	
AAS 'Twinkle Mix'			7"							Star patterned flowers fringed with pointed petals.	

*S = sun; PS = part shade; FS = full shade

Primula malacoides

Red salvia

Name	Season-Warm or Cool	Season of Bloom	Form	Color	Exposure* S	PS	FS	Days to Germination	Sowing to flower (weeks)	Comments	Uses
PORTULACA	W	S, F	6" trailing	Red, pink, rose, lavender, yellow, white, red	●			10	8	Thrives in hot dry locations; prolific flowering.	In shallow pots and containers. Hanging baskets.
Single or double flowered varieties				Individual or mixed colors							
PRIMULA	C	W, Sp	5-20"	Red, pink, rose, lavender, purple, blue, white shades	●	●		5-8 mo. seed to flower	21-28	Not heat tolerant; in cold winter areas use indoors; many species available.	Edge, pots, hanging bouquet.
P. malacoides Fairy Primrose			5-15"							Faster to flower; non-irritating foliage; includes 'Rhinepearl.'	
P. obconica			8-15"							Long bloom; foliage may cause skin irritation.	
SALVIA	W	S, F	6-30" erect and bushy	Scarlet-red, white, pink, blue	●	●		12-15	8-10	Grown for its bright red flower spikes. Dwarf forms are best for containers. Will not tolerate full shade or cold.	Grow in large pots and boxes. Strong color. Cool it down with white petunias.
'Scarlet Pygmy'			6"	Scarlet						Early flowering on compact, rounded plants.	
'Hot Jazz'			14"	Dark scarlet-red						Large dark green leaves. Tightly flowered spike.	
'St. Johns Fire'			12"	Scarlet-red						Early, heavy bloom on a small compact plant.	
SNAPDRAGON	C-W	Sp, S, F	6-36"	Many red, pink, rose, orange, yellow, bronze, lavender, shades and white	●			7-14	14	Dwarf forms best in containers. In mild winter areas a late summer sowing produces winter bloom. Cut back spikes after flowering for continuous bloom.	Dwarf types give good show in planters. Excellent cut flower.
'Floral Carpet'			7"	Many of above						Mound-shaped plants producing many 3" spikes. Long bloom.	
AAS 'Little Darling'			15"	Many of above						Open flowers (snapless). Compact base-branching plants with profuse bloom.	
SWEET PEAS	W	Sp, S	8-36" mounds or climbing vine	White, red, pink, blue, lavender shades and white	●			15	16	Small bush types best for containers. Profuse bloomers. Generally heat sensitive.	Grow in large pots and tubs. Good cut flower.
'Bijou'			15" bush type	All of above						Early, heat resistant plant covered with long stemmed, ruffled flowers.	
'Knee High'			30" will climb	All of above						Compact. Heat resistant. Large flowers.	
'Little Sweetheart'			8" bush type	All of above						Compact, bushy mounds covered with ruffled flowers.	

*S = sun; PS = part shade; FS = full shade

Dwarf snapdragon

Verbena

Zinnia bed

Name	Season-Warm or Cool	Season of Bloom	Form	Color	Exposure* S	Exposure* PS	Exposure* FS	Days to Germination	Sowing to flower (weeks)	Comments	Uses
THUNBERGIA	W	S, F	Trailing vine	Orange, yellow, white with black throat	●			12	12-16	Dense foliage. Profuse blooms. Will overwinter in mild areas.	Trailers for hanging baskets.
T. alata 'Alta' (Black Eyed Susan)				All of above						1-inch wide flowers.	
T. gibsanii 'Orange Lantern'				Orange with black throat						2-inch wide flowers.	
TORENIA	W	S, F	8" mounds	White or violet-blue with golden yellow throat		●		15	12-16	Compact bushy plants. *Fournieri compacta* is the available form.	Use in pots and window boxes. Combine with lobelia, small ferns.
VERBENA	W	S, F	4-20" spreading mounds	Red, pink, blue, purple, white shades some with white centers	●			20	10-12	Compact bush type best for containers. Drought tolerant. Profuse bloomer in hot climates.	A native American plant with about the truest red, white, and blue colors available in bedding plants. Vibrant clusters of flowers stand out in pots, window boxes or hanging baskets. Full sun.
AAS 'Blaze'			8"	Scarlet						Excellent compact habit. Dark green foliage. Large flowers.	
AAS 'Amethyst'			8"	Blue						Same fine habit as above.	
'Sparkle Mix'			8"	All colors mostly with white centers						Same plant form as 'Amethyst' and 'Blaze'	
'Rainbow Mix'			8"	Mixed most with white centers						More upright than others. Ideal for pots.	
VINCA (Periwinkle) *Vinca rosea* Madagascar periwinkle	W	S, F		Red, pink, rose, white with contrasting center	●	●		15	12-14		This is the annual Vinca, not to be confused with the perennial groundcover (Vinca major, V. minor). Bright phlox-like flowers stand out against glossy foliage. Best in pots and boxes.
Border Type			10"							Compact habit; includes 'Little Blanche,' 'Little Bright Eye,' 'Little Pinkie,' 'Little Delicata.'	
AAS 'Polka Dot'			6" trailing	White with red center							
ZINNIA	W	S, F	6-30" erect	Wide range of single and bicolors	●			7	8	Many sizes and flower forms. Best in heat.	Taller varieties can be massed in large containers for showy display and cut flowers. Shorter, bushier varieties excellent for potted color in full, hot sun.
AAS 'Buttons'			10"	Pink, red, yellow shades						Compact habit. Covered with double flowers.	
AAS 'Peter Pan'			12"	Orange, scarlet, rose, pink, cream						Compact. Large double flowers impressive in pots.	
AAS 'Thumbe-lina'			6"	Complete range						Double flowers appear when plants are only 4" tall. Long blooming season.	

*S = sun; PS = part shade; FS = full shade

Hanging baskets of fibrous begonias.

What's new and colorful?

In the garden world there's an annual colorful pageant—first the great seed farms, then the nursery green houses, then into the seed catalogs, and finally in pots, boxes, and borders in instant color everywhere. This is the ritual of renewal of our most colorful plants. And in this ritual "new" plants, and "new" colors and forms of old plants are selected and scientifically engineered. In this book we pay tribute to all members of the pageant.

As this book goes to press we have looked at the pageant of this year. In making judgments about the performance of the new introductions offered in future years we reserve the right to change our mind. A new introduction may hold its popularity for many years, or for months.

Box and pot gardening make comparative trial plantings easy to handle. One or two plants of a new variety, or variety you haven't tried, compared to the variety you have been growing will tell you whether or not the new ones will grow in your garden as advertised.

Anyway, here is how we judge some of the newcomers to the old-favorites group.

Begonias

'Glamour'—A new addition to the large-flowered fibrous rooted begonias. The flowers are larger than any other varieties in its class and appear when the plants are only 3-inches high. In our own test garden 'Glamour's' compact growth habit, prolific flowering, and glossy, waxy foliage have made it a favorite. Grown in the flowerbed they'll reach a height of 10 Inches, but in a pot will stay a compact 6-8 inches. After four months of growth our 'Glamours' are still compact, never having been pinched, in 4-inch pots. The 'Glamour' begonias have excellent heat tolerance, an understandable trait, having been developed in the heat of the Florida sun.

Carnations

'Juliet'—Grown in test gardens across the country the performance of this variety merited an award from the All-America Selection Committee. The flowers are fully double, measuring 2½-inches in diameter with a bright scarlet-red color. Their uniformity in trial grounds is most impressive—they all seem to be exactly 12-inches high.

You can see at a glance that this compact carnation would look good massed in a large container.

Dahlias

The dahlia enthusiast may look with little respect at the quick growing dahlia from seed. There have been a lot of changes made, however, since the days of 'Unwin' dwarf seed dahlias. Now the plant breeder offers the choice of colorful compact varieties.

New on the dahlia scene is 'Rigoletto.' This variety has already generated enthusiasm among the commercial growers due to its earliness (one week earlier than 'Early Bird') and compact habit. Another major attraction is its higher percentage of double flowers than any of the other existing varieties. The brightly colored flowers are produced on 15-inch tall, well-branched plants. When grown in pots, 'Rigoletto' will maintain a compact 12-inch tall habit.

The fibrous begonia 'Glamour.'

'Sprinter Deep Red' geranium.

'Sprinter Salmon'

Fibrous begonias — new and old

VARIETY	COLOR	COMMENT
Dwarf 6-8"		
Linda	deep rose	very free flowering, compact, and weather resistant
Viva	pure white	same excellent qualities as 'Linda'
Scarletta	scarlet-red	excellent habit, darker foliage than above
White Tausendschon	white	compact and early, profuse bloom
Derby	white edged, salmon	uniform, compact, and early
Comets	red, rose, pink, white, and 'Galaxy Mix'	bronze foliage, compact all season, white may be taller
Cocktail Mix	'Gin'-pink, 'Vodka'-scarlet-red, 'Whiskey'-white	bronze foliage, compact and sun resistant
Electra	light scarlet tinged salmon	weather resistant and early
Intermediate 8-10"		
Pink Tausendschon	pink	very free flowering
Red Tausendschon	red	bronze-green foliage, free flowering
Organdy Mix	red, rose and pink	20% bronze foliage soft colors
Othello	scarlet-orange	bronze foliage, good in pots or in the garden
Tall 12-14"		
Caravelle Series	red, rose, pink	well shaped, large leaves, must be pinched
Fortuna	rose, scarlet	large flowered and bushy, taller than above
Danica	rose, scarlet	similar to 'Fortuna' but bronze foliage
Cinderella	rose, white, with yellow center	50% large and 50% small flowers

Geraniums

What is it about a bushy red geranium in a moss-covered pot that seems to say "gardening"? Geraniums have been popular in homes and gardens since before the American Revolution. They have gone through many changes in breeding; improving the plant and flower greatly, but the geranium still retains its old-fashioned quality. Versatility and a failure-proof reputation have always been their big appeal.

In recent years geranium breeders have finally perfected strains which grow "true" from seed. Geraniums are as easy to grow from seed as they are from cuttings. The added advantage of starting geraniums from seed is their use as an annual in the spring and summer garden. Most varieties require about 120 days from seed to first bloom, so start seed indoors in February for mid-July bloom. These geraniums will bloom freely until frost at which time they can be potted up and brought indoors for winter color.

Comparing both the cutting varieties and the seed varieties of geraniums side by side in field plantings, we gave the nod to the seed-grown varieties for their bushy habit and long flowering period. Some of the leading varieties among the seed geraniums are the 'Carefree' series and 'Sprinter' series. The Sprinter series now includes 'Sprinter Deep Red,' 'Sprinter Salmon,' and 'Sprinter White.'

Many varieties of
impatiens displaying
their best in
containers and
hanging baskets.

'Fancifrills' is the new
double-flowered
impatiens.

'Futura,' a new
variety of impatiens.

Impatiens varieties

VARIETY	COLOR	COMMENT
Dwarf Single Color 6-10"		
Elfin Series	Pink, white, orange, salmon, rose, red, mix	basal branching, no pinching needed, very dwarf, free flowering and large early bloom
Grande Mix	wide range	'Elfin' like habit, dwarfer than other large flowered forms
Babies	orange, pink, scarlet, white, scarlet/orange, mix	compact, very dwarf, flat growth, foliage color varies, free flowering
Dwarf Bicolors 6-10"		
General Guisan (A-Go-Go)	scarlet red and white	neat habit, deep green foliage, hybrid has better form than inbred
Stars and Stripes	scarlet, rose, pink, crimson, orange, salmon, bicolored white	good dwarf habit, bronze foliage, flowers blotched or striped white
Zig-Zag	rose, scarlet, salmon, pink, orange, bicolored white	similar to Imps in habit
Semi-Dwarf Single Colors 12-15"		
Imp Series	carmine, pink, orange, purple, rose, scarlet, white, salmon, mix	uniform, well branched habit, large flowers, hardy, good in difficult shaded area
Minette Series	orange, salmon, rose/pink, white, scarlet, mix	basal branching, no pinching needed, Elfin bloom with more vigor
Tangeglow	bright orange	free flowering, dark, glossy foliage, large flowers with rich color
Semi-Dwarf Bicolors 12-15"		
Ripple Series	rose, scarlet, orange, fuchsia, bicolored white	good dwarf branching habit, large bloom, clear star pattern

Impatiens

A shade-lover that will add color to areas where other annuals wouldn't dare spread their roots. Impatiens make a magnificent display in hanging baskets as well as other containers. Never to complain, they will tolerate dry conditions and low soil fertility. There are many varieties available offering a wide range of colors, and various plant heights to choose from. Some unique additions to this variety list are the following new varieties:

'Fancifrills'—Available only as plants, this unique variety offers brightly colored, double flowers on 15-inch tall plants. Their well formed buds give the appearance of small rosebuds. They can be grown in a 4 or 5-inch pot if pinched regularly to stimulate branching. In the flowerbed they provide an unusual display of color.

'Twinkles'—A variegated flowered impatiens with a red and white bicolor pattern. Its variegated pattern is more distinct than most other variegated varieties. The compact plant habit of 'Twinkles' makes it adaptable to pots and baskets as well as flowerbeds.

'Futura'—Brightly colored flowers are produced on compact plants. Has large flowers which provide a striking color display in the flowerbed or in a hanging basket. (See photo.)

A small display of marigolds can be as impressive as a bigger one in the entryway above.

Marigolds

It's difficult for plant breeders to improve on the fool-proof performance of the existing marigold varieties, but recently worthy contributions have been made in the triploid hybrid group. The performance of these hybrids is impressive; they stand up to intense summer heat and heavy rains. Here are a few additions to the chart in the triploid hybrid class:

'Legal Gold'—Prolific flowering on stocky 12-inch tall plants. The flowers are double with a 2½-inch diameter and are gold in color. An excellent pot plant.

'Red Nugget'—A red flowered addition to the existing 'Nugget' series. The flowers are double, 2 inches in diameter, and are produced on compact plants, which grow only 10 inches tall in pots.

Snapdragons

'Pixie Mix'—This dwarf snapdragon is in the "open flower class" (snapless) and offers a color blend of orange, pink, red, white, and yellow flowers. In the garden it will reach a height of 6-8 inches. Excellent for growing in 4-inch pots.

Zinnias

'Pink Ruffles'—An excellent companion to 'Scarlet Ruffles,' a recipient of an All-America gold medal. The double pink flowers are produced on well-branched 24-30-inch plants. One of the major attributes of these varieties are their long stems which makes them excellent for cut flowers. We've seen both these varieties growing in various trial grounds and were impressed by their excellent flower form and prolific flowering. If you have a place for a large tub or box, 'Pink Ruffles' makes an interesting container choice.

Marigold height and form

When measuring the height of marigolds grown in our test gardens, we were surprised at how often we agreed with the height listed in nursery catalogs. Variations in the hybrids was much less than in the inbreds. All of the tall varieties grew taller than cataloged.

Variety	Height	Flower	Type — Comments
Petite Gold*	6"	Fully double 1¼" golden flowers on compact mounds.	Petite series. French type. Series including 'Petite Orange' AAS, 'Petite Yellow,' and 'Petite Mix.'
Petite Spry	7"	Double red with yellow crest.	
Petite Harmony*	8"	Mahogany red and orange.	
Brownie Scout	8"	Fully double 1¼" Gold splashed with red.	French type with petite mound habit.
Lemon Drop	6-8"	Fully double 1¼" lemon yellow.	Petite mound habit.
Yellow Nugget	10-12"	Double 2¼" flowers. Triploid.	Nugget series. Also includes: 'Orange Nugget,' 'Gold Nugget' and mixed colors.
Pumpkin Crush	10-12"	Huge, fully double 4½" orange blooms.	Guys and Dolls series. Also offered as yellow, gold, and mixed varieties.
Aztec	10-12"	Gold, yellow orange, mix 3-4" flowers.	Double Carnation type.
Bolero*	10-12"	Fully double 2½" flowers. Bright maroon, gold center.	Double French bicolor.
Honeycomb	10-12"	Fully double 1½" crested blooms. Maroon petals, gold border.	Royal Crested series, also includes the bicolors 'Autumn Haze,' 'Gold Rush' and 'Star Dust.'
Gold Cupid	10-12"	Mumlike 2½" blooms.	Cupid series includes: orange, yellow and mix varieties.
Spanish Brocade	10-12"	Gold and deep red blooms.	Semi-double French bicolor. Very early.
Fiesta	12"	Carnation type crimson and yellow.	Olé series includes 'Matador' and 'Picador.'
Tiger	12-15"	Closely packed petals of bright gold.	A triploid hybrid with extra long flowering period. Earliest of the group.
Showboat*	13"	2½" golden yellow	Triploid hybrid.
Harvest Moon	14"	Crested 1½" orange blooms.	Moon series also includes: 'Honey,' 'Honey Moon' (yellow). Blooms at 6".
Rusty Red	14"	Well doubled 2½" rusty mahogany blooms.	Becomes marked with gold as it matures.
Gold Galore*	14-16"	Double carnation type 3¼" golden yellow.	Densely branched, compact bush.
First Lady*	18"	Double carnation type 3¼" yellow.	Lady series. Includes 'Gold Lady' and 'Orange Lady.' Hedge type. Erect, bushy, rounded.
Naughty Marietta	18-20"	2" single golden yellow with red eye.	Also 'Dainty Marietta,' lower growing to 12".
Senator Dirksen	24"	Double carnation type 3½" golden yellow.	Hedge type. Very vigorous. They were 34" tall in our garden.
Orange Hawaii	30-36"	Double carnation type 4" blooms.	Odorless foliage. Carnation flowered. Series includes 'Golden Hawaii.'
Yellow Crackerjack	30-36"	Double carnation type 5" blooms.	Crackerjack series. Also offered as orange, gold, and mix. Erect, bushy.
Yellow Doubloon	36"	Extra double 3½-4" carnation type blooms.	Gold Coin series. Includes: 'Sovereign' (gold), 'Double Eagle' (orange).
Yellow Climax	36"	Fully double carnation type 5" ruffled, globular blooms.	Climax series. Includes 'Golden,' 'Primrose' (creamy), 'Toreador' (AAS, deep orange) and mixed. Sturdy, erect, bushy.

*AAS

Achimenes are
excellent winter pot
plant or for shady
hanging baskets.

The fluffy look of
Asparagus meyeri.

Italian bellflower
(Campanula
isophylla).
See text.

Plants that drape and trail

In the chart of annual plants for containers, hanging
baskets, and hanging bouquets we list many plants which
will perform briefly in hanging baskets. Here we add to the
list the bulbs, vines, groundcovers, and shrubs which
have the hanging basket habit of growth.

Achimenes. A tender flowering bulb for spring and summer color. Excellent for hanging baskets or other containers in partially shaded locations. The 'Cascade' varieties
are exceptional for hanging basket displays. Flower color
includes blue, pink, rose, purple, light yellow, orange,
crimson, and red. Plant 3-5 bulbs per 12″ basket .The bulbs
will require a few months rest period, after the foliage dies;
store in a cool, dry location for the winter months.

Basket-of-Gold (Alyssum saxatile). A hardy perennial that
will provide color in spring and early summer. Hang it in
full sun for a mass display of golden yellow color. Good
combination with other sun-loving plants. After blooming,
lightly trim the plants, removing no more than half the
growth. Hardy all areas.

Asparagus fern. The asparagus ferns are not true ferns
but they provide as equally attractive display of foliage as

their namesake. Of the group, the best for hanging baskets is the 'Spenger' asparagus with its arching stems
providing a cascading display of lush, green color. Its
needlelike foliage is heavily textured and borne in clusters
along the stems. Plant is a vigorous grower and requires
periodic pruning of old stems to provide room for new
shoots. Grow in full sun or partial shade where summers
are hot. Bring indoors in cold winter areas. Hardy to 20°.

Aubrieta (Aubrieta deltoidea). Aubrieta is a low growing
perennial with silver green foliage and spring flowers of
red, pink, or lavender. It requires light shearing after flowering, with never more than half the growth cut back.
A sunny exposure is best, except in hot areas where
partial shade should be provided. A good combination
plant with Basket-of-Gold. Hardy all areas.

Begonia, tuberous (B. tuberhybrida 'pendula'). There are
a wide variety of glamorous flower forms and colors in this
special group designated as 'Hanging Basket Begonias.'
Colors include white, yellow, pink, orange, red, and various
bi-color patterns. They will flower from summer to fall in
partial or full shade. The begonia tubers must be dug up
at the end of the flowering season and stored in a cool,
dry location until it is time for next season's planting.

Hanging baskets of fuchsias and tuberous begonias thrive in the cool shade of this garden deck.

Bougainvillea. This showy plant performs best in warm-winter climates, but can be adapted to colder areas if given winter protection. In areas of frequent frost keep it protected against a warm wall, or move indoors. Grow in partial shade where summer temperatures are high; otherwise in full sun. Pinch frequently to encourage bushiness. 'Crimson Jewel' makes a good hanging basket specimen with dark green leaves and masses of glowing red flowers.

Camellia *(C. hiemalis).* Two varieties, formerly in the *C. sasanqua* class, 'Showa-No-Sakae' (pink semi-double flowers) and 'Shishi-Gashira' (rose-red double flowers) make attractive hanging basket plantings. Both have graceful arched branch patterns and bloom over a long period between October and March. Flower production is reduced by a combination of cold weather and abundant rain. In parts of the South where these conditions exist, grow camellias under an overhang, or similar protection, for best bloom.

Italian bellflower *(Campanula isophylla).* This long-time favorite for hanging baskets flowers vigorously in late summer and fall in shades of lavender, blue, and white. Dense foliage hangs down 18-24 inches. 'Alba' is a popular white variety; 'Mayi,' a blue one.

Cotoneaster. There are a number of species within the cotoneaster group, two of which are well adapted for growing in baskets. The creeping cotoneaster *(C. adpressa)* is a slow growing, deciduous shrub that grows to a height of 12 inches and bears pink flowers followed by bright red berries. Also providing a cascading display of flowers (white) and red berries is the bearberry cotoneaster *(C. dammeri).* It has evergreen foliage and reaches a height of 6 inches. Grow in full sun or partial shade. Hardy all areas.

Kenilworth ivy *(Cymbalaria muralis).* A perennial vine for hanging in partially shaded locations. Its small leaves are somewhat kidney shaped and borne close together along trailing stems. Flowers are small, lilac-blue with white and yellow markings, and appear from spring to fall. Commonly grown as an annual in cold winter areas.

Euonymus. Many varieties of *E. fortunei* serve well as hardy groundcovers and their wide speading habit makes them useful in hanging baskets. Keep wayward branches pruned when grown in hanging baskets. The purple-leaf, wintercreeper variety, 'Colorata' will drape nicely, as will the green and white variegated form 'Gracillis.' Grow in full sun or partial shade. Hardy all areas.

When Fuchsias are grown outside their preferred cool summer, the important thing is to give them protection from hot winds.

Shore Juniper drapes from hanging basket.

Fuchsia. Selected varieties of fuchsias are at the top of the list for hanging basket plants. In the hot summer areas, fuchsia enthusiasts resort to mist spraying to give the fuchsia the climate it needs. They will survive a light frost, although leaves and young growth will be injured. In hard frost areas treat as an annual, take cuttings for next spring, or bring entire plant indoors. Spring is the time for pruning, cutting back approximately the amount of growth made the previous summer, or removing frost injured wood. Blooms early, summer to frost. Hang baskets in a location protected from wind and in partially shaded exposure.

Gardenia 'Radicans.' This gardenia grows to 6 to 12 inches high and spreads 2 to 3 feet. Flowers (1-inch) are smaller than the typical gardenia, but have the same fragrance. Needs summer heat for best performance. Grow in part shade in hot summer areas; full sun in the cooler climates.

Ivy (Hedera helix). The trailing habit of this woody vine has made it popular as a container plant indoors and out. It is available in a wide variety of leaf shapes, sizes, and colors. The small leaved varieties of 'Baltic ivy,' 'Pixie' and 'Needlepoint' are popular hanging basket varieties. Don't hesitate to take cuttings from your ivy and grow them in the same pot. Hardy all areas.

Candytuft (Iberis sempervirens). Not to be confused with its annual cousin, this evergreen perennial makes an attractive basket with its foliage serving as a contrasting background for its snow white flowers. Flowering occurs in early spring and literally covers the plant. After flowering a light trimming will stimulate compact growth. It prefers full sun although partial shade is also suitable. Hardy all areas.

Juniper. As ground covers the low growing junipers grow wide—up to 10 feet. Several of the spreading types will spill and drape in hanging baskets. Shore juniper (J. conferta) is a natural trailer, adapted to seashore conditions, but also has good heat tolerance in interior conditions. Bar Harbor juniper (J.h 'Bar Harbor') is fast growing. Will spread 10 feet when planted in the open. Greyish-blue foliage turns plum-colored with cold weather. Andorra juniper (J.h. plumosa) is a wide spreading juniper with a flat branching habit. Grey-green foliage turns plum in winter. Blue Carpet juniper (J.h. Wiltonii) is a very low growing juniper with striking silver-blue color. Juniper procumbens 'Nana' has artistic heavy branches with irregular growth. Stubby, dense, blue-green foliage. Check other low-growing junipers for hanging basket possibilities.

Ivy makes great hanging basket material . . .

. . . or it can be trained in many ways. This patio umbrella is a unique example.

Ivy will willingly follow your lead.

Lantana *(Lantana montevidensis).* In mild winter areas this trailing shrub can add year round color to the container garden. Plants are easily damaged by light frosts, but usually survive to give a full bloom the following year—just trim out dead wood to maintain neat appearance. Some of the more colorful varieties are 'Gold Mound' (yellow-orange), 'Confetti' (pink, yellow and purple) and 'Carnival' (crimson, lavender, yellow and pink). Grow in full sun. Hardy 20-24°.

Parrot's beak. The stems of this finely textured, grey foliaged plant droop 24-36 inches. Small scarlet flowers appear in abundance in mid-summer. Trim to prevent ''legginess'' and protect from winter cold. Enjoys full sun. Hardy to 26-28°.

Moneywort *(Lysimachia nummularia).* Popular for its foliage as well as its golden yellow flowers. It's a hardy perennial which can be grown in sun or shade. The trailing stems will produce a cascading display of foliage and flowers in spring and summer. Hardy all areas.

Geranium, ivy *(Pelargonium peltatum).* An attractive vining plant with glossy leaves and numerous round flower clusters of pink, red, white, or lavender. Grows well in full sun

in cool climates, but should be grown in partial shade in hot summer areas. In hard frost areas treat as an annual, or bring the plant indoors and place in a bright window for the winter. 'Sybil Holmes' (pink) and 'Mrs. Banks' (white with purple markings) are popular basket varieties. Hardy to 10-20°.

Stonecrop *(Sedum sieboldii).* An interesting hanging display is provided by the thick, red margined leaves and bright pink flowers. Its dense flower clusters provide fall color. Grow in a sunny location and keep on the dry side. Completely hardy.

Periwinkle, Myrtle *(Vinca major, V. minor).* Commonly, and effectively grown as a ground cover, these hardy vines provide an attractive display of draping foliage and 1-2 inch blue flowers in the spring. A variegated form of the large leafed *V. major* is available. There's a white flower form of the dwarf periwinkle. Of the two, the *V. minor* is the hardier. Both will grow in sun or shade.

Ways with trees and shrubs

Growing trees and shrubs in boxes is not a new idea. In Egypt, about 4,000 years ago, trees were grown in large

The Japanese Garden juniper in its compact form (J. procumbens 'nana') is hanging basket material.

A dwarf Alberta spruce that has been left in its original nursery can since 1958.

Variegated Pieris, dwarfed by long life in a nursery can, is reborn and raised high with a ground cover of "Blue Star Creeper."

"boxes" or "pots" cut in rock and filled with special soil. According to the best of records, commercial nurserymen brought Frankincense trees in containers from the Somali Coast to Egypt, to be grown in local gardens, about 3,500 years ago.

A walk through a modern nursery with container-use in mind will discover that all plants can be grown in containers—at least in their youthful stages. Remember that growth in containers can be controlled and disciplined. Slow growing shrubs and trees are the logical choices, and will accept container conditions for years.

The shrubs and trees in the following lists have the proper container qualifications.

Shrubs for containers

Glossy Abelia *(A. grandiflora)* — Evergreen to semi-deciduous. Colorful combination of foliage and flower. New leaves coppery, gradually turn glossy green. Arching branches. Flower clusters white to pinkish-white from early summer into fall. Prune selectively in late winter. For best color grow in full sun. Hardy to 0°.

Purple Leaf Japanese Barberry *(Berberis thunbergii 'Atropurpurea')* — Deciduous. A good portable barrier valued for its finely textured colorful foliage. Leaves bronzy-red spring and summer. Yellow, orange, and red in fall. Red berries revealed after leaves drop. Dense habit. Branches arching, heavily thorned. Can be sheared, but more attractive when selectively pruned. Grow in full sun. Hardy to —20°.

Natal Plum *(Carissa grandiflora)* — Evergreen. The Natal Plum is one of the few shrubs that puts on a year 'round show. Large (2 inch) star shaped white flowers born throughout the year with a wonderful jasmine-like fragrance. Fruits (1-2 inches) are bright red, edible. Taste somewhat like sweet cranberries; used in sauces, jams, and pies. Leaves leathery, slightly glossy. Branches thorned. Easily trained into formal shapes. 'Boxwood Beauty' and 'Tomilson' are extremely compact, thornless varieties. Hardy to 25°.

Hinoki False Cypress *(Chamaecyparis obtusa)* — Evergreen. Slow to outgrow its place and easily kept below 6 feet. Can be trained to reveal its attractive, irregular branching pattern. The Dwarf Hinoki Cypress *(C.o. 'Nana')*, growing only 3 feet high, is round-headed with deep green foliage on layered branches. The Golden Hinoki Cypress

A juniper which might have been overlooked in its nursery can . . .

. . . but was replanted in a small container and took on a "bonsai" look. See chapter on Bonsai, page 70

A gardenia trained as standard lends a special elegance to this patio.

(*C.o. 'Aurea'*) has golden new foliage—gradually turns deep green. All Hinoki False Cypress make excellent bonsai specimens. Unsatisfactory in hot summer areas. Hardy to 10°.

Cleyera japonica — Evergreen. Slow growing shrub (6-8 feet), handsomely clothed in colorful foliage on gracefully arching branches. New leaves born brownish-red, gradually turn lustrous deep green, retaining a red midrib. Small clusters of fragrant white flowers in spring, followed by dark-red berries lasting into winter. Grow as you would its relative, the Camellia. Hardy to 0°.

Silverberry (*Elaegnus pungens*) — Evergreen. The grey-green foliage of this plant adds a silvery sparkle wherever it's used. Brownish flecks on leaves and stem reflect sunlight. Naturally a low growing, sprawling shrub, but is easily kept neat by pruning. Makes a tough container plant, good for wind and sun protection. Available in variegated leaf forms. Hardy to 15°.

Gardenia (*G. jasminoides*) — Evergreen. The gardenia's special style is accented when they're grown in containers and placed up front in entrance ways, decks, or patios. Waxy white flowers are beautifully fragrant, especially noticeable in the evening hours. Blooms late spring into summer, and occasionally throughout the year in mild climates. Leaves glossy green. Grows best in filtered shade, but will take full sun with ample moisture. Requires summer heat for best bloom. Hardy to 20°.

Chinese Hibiscus (*H. rosa-sinensis*) — Evergreen. A generous performer of summer color with large, showy flowers 4-8 inches), single or double, in many colors. Glossy leaves. Many varieties; choose for flower color and plant habit. Warm weather and sun will yield best bloom; needs afternoon shade in hottest areas. Cold sensitive (hardy to 20° with overhead protection). Bring indoors in cold winter areas.

Holly (*Ilex*) — Evergreen. Their glossy green foliage and bright red berries are a classic reminder of the holiday season. For large, long lasting berries on a slow growing compact plant, the Chinese holly (*Ilex cornuta*) 'Burfordii Nana' is a prime selection. It has the added attractions of being self-pollinating and spineless; (hardy to 0°). Less tolerant of dry heat, but equally fine container subjects are the many forms of English holly (*I. aquafolium*) (hardy to 0°). Actually resembling the Boxwood more than the familiar

Mugho pine is transformed by transplanting from box to bowl.

The fern-like, almost feathery, leaves of the silk tree give it a soft, gentle feeling.

Christmas holly, the Japanese holly *(I. crenata)* is the hardiest of the group (to −10°). Bears black berries. 'Compacta' is a particularly dense variety requiring little pruning. Grow all varieties in sun or partial shade. Prune to shape. Fine tied to a trellis, or as an espalier.

Mugho Pine *(Pinus mugo mughus)* — Evergreen. Kept small by pinching out new soft green shoots (candles) to 1-inch in spring, this pine is an ideal candidate for containers. Pleasantly full, deep green foliage. Hardy in all areas.

Heavenly Bamboo *(Nandina domestica)* — Evergreen. A light airy shrub with an Oriental feel suggestive of bamboo. Many slender, unbranched stems, bearing softly textured leaves divided into leaflets. Foliage born pinkish-bronze, gradually turns green. Picks up a purple or bronze tinge in fall. Scarlet in winter sun. Grows 6-8 feet but easily controlled. Bright red berries in fall if male and female plants are used together. Hardy to 5°.

Japanese Black Pine *(Pinus thunbergiana)* — Evergreen. A favorite for bonsai training, equally valuable as a tub specimen. Slow growing; may take 3-4 years to reach 4 feet. Takes well to pruning. Hardy all areas.

Trees for containers

Looking down the list of trees we have selected as container subjects, you may find your favorite missing. We do not claim the list to be complete. We have limited our list to those trees which are worth the extra attention in pruning and shaping called for when displayed in a container.

Silk Tree *(Albizia julibrissin)*. Deciduous. A soft gentle feeling seems to prevail around this tree. Light green fern-like leaves seem infinitely divided, almost feathery. Light sensitive, they fold at night. Branches arch to form flat topped canopy providing excellent filtered shade. Pink flower puffs held above foliage in summer. Fast growing yet held to container size (10-15 ft.) for years.

Eastern Redbud *(Cercis candensis)*. Deciduous. For an early spring flower show the Redbud will satisfy even the most demanding observer. Small, pea-like, pink to purple or white flowers completely cover the leafless branches. Heart shaped leaves provide summer shade ideal for patios. Turn yellow in fall. Showy seed pods revealed in winter after leaves drop. Of the many varieties, 'Forest Pansy' is of interest with pinkish-purple flowers and purple leaves on red stems. 'Alba' is a white, profuse flowering variety.

Baby pines change color and character as they grow. The Japanese Black Pine (Pinus thunbergii), one of the favorite bonsai pines, is an excellent choice.

Rhododendrons can be trained as a patio plant.

Naked Coral Tree (*Erythrina coralloides*). Deciduous. This tree is an eye-catcher every season. Produces fiery red pinecone-like blossoms in spring. Large leaves provide summer shade before they turn yellow and drop in late autumn. In winter its interesting shape and branching pattern never go unnoticed.

Pineapple Guava (*Feijoa sellowiana*). Evergreen. Normally it grows as a dense gray-green shrub noteworthy for its flowers and fruit. Flowers are made up of 4 thick white petals, tinged purplish beneath, and a big tuft of bright red stamens. The fleshy petals are edible. The soft fruits, 2 to 4 inches long are filled with juicy, aromatic pulp.

At its best when pruned and trained as a picturesque small tree. Unusually hardy for a subtropical. Will take a 15° frost.

Sunburst Honey Locust (*Gleditsia triacanthos inermis* 'Sunburst'). Deciduous. This tree makes up for its lack of flower color with golden-yellow new foliage highlighted by the older, light green leaves. Overall effect of a wonderful yellow bloom from spring to fall. Leaves finely divided into small leaflets. Softly textured. Entire tree turns yellowish-gold in fall. Ideal for close quarters and containers.

Holly (*Ilex*). Evergreen. There are hollies that have no spines on the leaves and ones that don't look like "hollies." There are hollies with black fruits and red fruits. There are hollies that are low spreading dwarfs and kinds that are small trees. Here are a few of the most useful:

The Japanese holly (*Ilex crenata*) bears no resemblance to the Christmas holly. Even the berries are black. Many resemble boxwood more than they do the conventional holly.

The convex leaf holly, with its small leaves and dark green color is very amenable to shearing, and although it will grow to 8 feet or more, it can be held at any height.

The Chinese holly (*I. cornuta*) and its horticultural form, Burford Chinese holly, are at home in every mild-winter climate. The Burford holly has the elegance of an "entrance" shrub and the toughness of a weed in its ability to grow. Leaves of the Burford holly have almost no spines. It makes a compact shiny green shrub 6 to 9 feet high. Berries are bright red.

Yaupon holly (*I. vomitoria*) is a native of the South. It grows as a large shrub or small tree up to 20 feet high. Its red fruits are quite showy. Dwarf forms available.

Crape myrtle tree,
photographed at the
nursery in late
August.

Many strong
growing Southern
Indian azaleas
can be trained
as standards.

Golden Rain Tree *(Koelreuteria paniculata)*. Deciduous. Uncommon summer color abounds from this well behaved tree. Large clusters of yellow flowers in mid-summer. New foliage salmon in spring. Long leaves (12-15 inches) divided into leaflets. Fruits papery; Japanese lantern-like; good ornamental value lasting into winter. Fairly slow growth makes it a good container tree (10-15 ft.).

Crape Myrtle *(Lagerstroemia indica)*. Deciduous. In summer when flowering trees are hard to find, the crape myrtle comes across in style. Flowers crinkled, crepe-like in shades of white, pink, rose, or lavender. Blooms over a long period. Light green leaves turn orangish-red in fall. Mottled tan bark and branching is of winter interest.

The National Arboretum has developed a group of crape myrtles, called Indian Tribe, of superior hardiness, performance, and mildew resistance. Named varieties are: red flowering 'Cherokee,' purple flowering 'Catawba,' pink flowering 'Potomac' and 'Seminole,' and light lavender 'Powhatan.'

Glossy Privet *(Ligustrum lucidum)*. Evergreen. An admirable performer in large tubs reaching tree size quickly and thriving in tight quarters for years. Large feathery clusters

of white flowers in spring. Followed by dark blue fruits in quantity. Luxuriant, almost deep green, glossy foliage. Easily trained into many shapes, single or multi-trunked.

Magnolia. Evergreen. Few things are easier to live with than the spring elegance of the magnolia. Large (up to 10" across) fragrant flowers. Blooms spring to early summer in shades of white, pink, and purple. Interesting, colorful seed capsules follow flowers. Giant (up to 12" long by 5" wide), stiff, glossy green leaves.

Magnolias outgrow containers eventually but smaller, slow growing forms of Southern magnolia *(M. grandiflora)*, like 'St. Mary,' are handsome in boxes for years.

Oleander *(Nerium oleander)*. Evergreen. Trained as a single-trunked tree and placed in a container, this normally dense sprawling shrub will add color to the patio when tree color is hard to come by. Generous bloom from late spring to early fall, accented handsomely by somewhat leathery, dark green foliage. Choose from a wide range of colors—pink, rose, red, salmon, light yellow, and white. Foliage damaged at 10° but recovers in spring.

Palms. Evergreen. Several palms make very fine container trees. The Parlor Palm *(Chamaedorea elegans)* is slow

Containers of Dwarf Oleander fresh from the nursery are put into "quick-change" box along with 8 pots of marigolds.

Container grown wisteria vine trained as a large shrub.

growing to 3-4 feet; typical, fish skeleton-like leaves sheath the single trunk emerging in a cluster at the top. The Pygmy Palm *(Phoenix roebelenii)* grows to 6 feet. Its leaves are less airy and emerge from the top of the slender stem. The Paradise Palm *(Howea forsteriana)* has similar leaves on a clean stem (9 ft.) interestingly scarred. The Lady Palm *(Raphis excelsa)* is an old favorite in containers growing 6 to 12 feet tall. It yields a bushy, bamboo-like effect with many stalks bearing Oriental fan-like foliage at the tips.

Yew Pine *(Podocarpus macrophyllus)*. Evergreen. A gentle tree, easy to live with up close. Valuable indoors and out. Leaves long (4 inches) and narrow. Yellowish-green new foliage contrasts nicely with older dark green leaves. Yields fern-like effect. Slow growth. Good in containers.

Caroliniana Laurel Cherry *(Prunus caroliniana)*. Evergreen. No bright unusual colors, just a dense, glossy tree for a luxurious touch of green. Small white flowers in late winter or early spring. Black berries follow bloom. Easily trained into formal shapes. Single or multi-trunked. Two varieties ideal in containers are 'Bright-n-Tight' and 'Compacta.'

Evergreen Pear *(Pyrus kawakamii)*. Evergreen. Left untouched it becomes a sprawling shrub. Tied to a trellis or wire it can easily be tailored as an espalier. Staked, it makes a handsome single-trunked tree. Glossy green foliage is a year round attraction. Fragrant white flowers abundant in late winter or early spring. Fast growing. Heavy pruning reduces flowering.

Ternstroemia gymnanthera. Evergreen. Pleasant to be around and slow growing enough to be in a tub for a long time. Leaves born a showy, bronzish-red. Gradually turn anywhere from green to purplish-red depending on temperature and exposure. Deepest reds and purples from cool temperatures and full sun. Prune to shape. Inconspicuous, yet fragrant yellow flowers followed by yellow berries.

Wisteria. Deciduous. You'll find this vigorous vine trained as a small tree, single trunked with an umbrella-like top. The "tree" produces the same long, lovely clusters of blossoms which make this woody plant the "queen of the vines." Flowers fragrant; born in spring in shades of white, pink, and lavender. Leaves (12-18 inches long) divided into leaflets. Good in containers.

Nature's most astounding bonsai, the ancient Bristlecone Pine, is confined to arid, lofty mountain areas of the western United States. Dwarfed by nature these oldest living trees have survived storm, drought, fire and pestilence for more than a thousand years.

Bonsai—centuries old, nursery new

The horticultural art form known as bonsai and developed over many centuries by the Japanese, is finding more and more devotées in the United States. The word derived originally from two Chinese symbols—"bon" meaning tray or pot, and "sai" meaning to plant; hence, "bonsai," the word for container planting. It has come to mean a very special type of container gardening. The dwarfing of trees to reflect a miniature segment of nature has developed with its rules for shaping, potting, pruning and otherwise caring for these living sculptures.

It is understandable that different styles evolved, each with its own standards for "sculpturing" and displaying, according to the kind of tree and natural setting depicted. The style is dictated by the tree chosen for dwarfing. Each bonsai should look like its mature counterpart in miniature—a tiny reproduction of nature.

Bonsai is an appreciation for nature and a feeling for its many moods—its towering mountains, its windswept cliffs; its meadows and lagoons, its rushing rivers and its talkative brooks. It is truly an art form of three dimensions about which the Japanese have written scholarly volumes.

It is not the attempt here to offer a course in the Japanese art of bonsai; but to point the way to getting started in bonsai, and to dispel some false ideas about it.

Bonsai is not difficult; but these miniatures make certain demands. Because they are confined to living in an extremely restricted space, their needs are special and require routine care to maintain, both in form and in health. They need regular watering, for if allowed to dry out, they will surely die.

Heirloom Pieces

Don't let the age of the bonsai trees you may have seen discourage you. There are some in private Japanese collections both here and in Japan that are upwards of three hundred and fifty years old. These are treasures of rare value, cherished by their owners and passed on to each succeeding generation as living heirlooms. These venerable specimens are seen by only a privileged few.

There are some very good collections of representative bonsai, not comparatively old, in the Brooklyn Botanical Garden, the Arnold Arboretum of Massachusetts (the Larz Anderson Collection, over fifty years old), and the Huntington Botanical Garden's new collection, San Marino, California. Some excellent specimens—a few up to a hundred years and more—are exhibited by private collectors in some of the major horticulture shows in this country.

Bonsai can be any age. The quality of a bonsai does not relate to its age but to the fine abstraction of nature that has been created. You can actually begin to enjoy a bonsai of your own right away.

Because bonsai is a nature art, perhaps the best way for a beginning is to take a field trip for the purpose of careful observation. Begin to see the details of nature's art—the way a trunk slants; its angle of growth as it reaches for the sun; the size of its leaves in proportion to their numbers; their shapes, their placement along the stalk—alternating? opposite?; their depth of color, their texture and the shadow pictures they draw in the changing light. This is the true beginning for a hobby of bonsai. For remember, your subject will become a miniature sculpture of nature.

True Bonsai

As with other art forms, there are certain basic components that must be considered in their relationship to the artistic whole. The container and the tree have the same relationship as the frame to the painting. Like the frame, the container must never compete with the tree. Japanese bonsai containers are fine examples of the art of simplicity. The Japanese follow generally the rules of using a glazed container for flowering specimens, while choosing an unglazed one for foliage subjects.

In selecting the subject for your bonsai, the trunk should be your first consideration; for it is the basis around which all other aspects of the tree are to be developed.

Most Japanese bonsai are shaped from woody or semiwoody plant material. There are five classical styles of bonsai using single trunk trees as the subject. These are shown in the photos on the opposite page. This is the primary division of the art that we will use to open the door for you to the easier-than-you-think world of bonsai.

On pages 72, 73 we show the very basic means to growing true bonsai or pseudo-bonsai. This will help you get started.

However, the International Bonsai Society is growing in this country, with new chapters springing up in many areas. Although there are many books available, a greater degree of early success and self confidence can be achieved by seeking first-hand guidance from more experienced bonsai culturists, who are always happy to help a beginner and share their knowledge willingly. To obtain the address of the Akebono Bonsai Society or study group in your area, write to: Ben T. Suzuki, Nippon Bonsai Association, 608 N. 21st Street, Montebello, California 90640.

**Informal upright
style** *has a slightly
slanting trunk, as in
this juniper.*

**Formal upright
style.** *The straight
trunk of this Japa-
nese maple is dis-
played on a deck.*

Slanting style *of
this ancient-looking
California juniper
is suggestive of a
windswept slope.*

Cascading style,
*as its name implies,
has at least one
main branch that
falls well below the
level of the
container.*

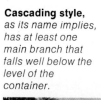

**Semi-cascading
styles** *make grace-
ful eye level
displays.*

How to get started with Bonsai

Containers for bonsai come in many sizes and shapes, some glazed and others unglazed; white, brown and some with subtle tones of sand and rock. Form of subject to be planted dictates the choice of pot.

You will need a few tools. Most nurseries and garden centers carry basic supplies including wire cutters, pruning shears and annealed copper wire—best for bonsai. Wire should be just slightly more rigid than the branches to be trained. Two or three sizes of dull pointed sticks (like chopsticks) for removing soil from roots and to untangle twisted ones.

Nursery stock offers the most available source of plants from which to start your first bonsai. Nursery discard plants with dwarfed trunks or irregular branching are just what the bonsai artist seeks. They are usually much cheaper, which adds to their appeal as good subjects for your first bonsai project.

A commercial nursery's procedure

We took our photographer to a wholesale nursery, Select Nurseries, Inc. in Brea, California, specialists in commercial bonsai production. The steps shown in the photos and in the following copy are the steps they use in creating bonsai. If you buy a tree in a gallon can at your nursery, you may follow the same procedure. A word of caution: *Don't work in the sun or wind*—roots dry out fast.

Step 1. Examine your subject, viewing it from all sides. Decide which should be the "front" side.

Step 2. Remove tree from container, holding trunk firmly at the base. Use a long knife or spatula to loosen root ball from sides. Tap gently, patiently to loosen from the bottom.

Step 3. Begin at the base of the tree and prune unwanted branches and stems. Eliminate *opposite* branching. Strive for *alternate* branches and alternate stems on the branches for an assymetric form. Remove growth from *underside* of branches.

Prune so that light will strike all branches equally. Proper pruning assists in getting good ventilation to all areas of your tree.

Step 4. In order to shape branches you must wire them. (A visit to a nursery or garden center where bonsai are displayed will show you how plants are shaped and how wire is used.)

It helps to practice the wiring technique on some scrap branches, so you get the feeling of bending a branch and noting its flexibility or rigidity.

Now get ready to wire your bonsai. Measure off lengths of wire equal to the length of the branch(es) plus at least a third more.

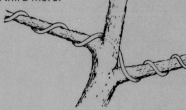

One wire may hold two branches if they are close on the trunk. Wrap the wire clockwise on one side; counterclockwise on the other side. This prevents the wire from girdling the trunk as the plant grows.

Anchor the wire at the base of a single branch by overlapping it.

Soil

Near the base of the plant the wire may be anchored in the soil.

Convex

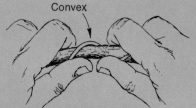

When bending a branch, be sure that thumbs brace *under* the curve where the wire wraps convexly or you might snap the branch and ruin the form of the tree.

When you reach the tip of the branch with the wiring, snip off any excess wire and bend backward and in close to the stem of the branch.

Don't wrap too tightly. Branches must have growing room. Wire is not applied to restrict growth—only for shaping. Wires that bite into bark make ugly marks that last for years.

Step 5. To prepare the tree for its new container, you'll need the following equipment: a pruning shears, dull-pointed sticks (like chopsticks), a pail of water to which a few drops of a chemical "starter solution" has been added, potting mix (see page 8 on soils), and a bonsai container with window screen mesh to cover drainage holes.

First, the root ball must be greatly reduced. If the root ball is a tangled mass of roots, use the chopstick to remove soil and untangle the snarl of roots girdling the ball. Don't damage new feeder roots. (They're the small, light-colored ones.) Older roots are thicker, often wiry and usually much darker. *Roots should spread in all four directions evenly.* Prune a third of all long, older roots you untangled.

Keep feeder roots moist by frequently dipping into the pail of water. Work quickly but carefully.

When one-third of the total root ball is removed, place tree in bonsai container that has a thick layer of potting mix in the bottom. If container is oval or oblong shape, place tree off-center about two-thirds the distance from the edge, allowing longest branch to spread directly above surface area, the shorter branch spread directly over the other

third. A square or round container usually calls for a center placement.

Holding tree with one hand, settle root ball into soil; use stick to spread roots around base evenly.

Sprinkle more soil over roots, covering them and pressing soil down to fill in all spaces between roots. Firm soil around them.

If necessary to get a stubborn root to stay down, a short length of wire can be bent to form a hairpin shape, then placed over the root and firmed into the soil to hold the root in place. This can be removed later, once the root has established itself in the soil.

Next set container in water until top of soil is moist. Add a top dressing, such as moss or pebbles.

Now is the time to make any changes in the direction of your branches by bending them carefully. You are the sculptor.

Display your finished sculpture in filtered, not direct, sun. Mist foliage. To maintain your bonsai, don't allow it to dry out. Pinch off new growth that is unwanted before it becomes woody. This will avoid heavy pruning.

Pseudo-bonsai

This method is for the imaginative and creative gardener without enough time for the more exacting art of true bonsai. The busy urbanite, or weekend gardener, may prefer to try pseudo-bonsai for instant effect before plunging into the more painstaking horticultural processes involved in the art of true bonsai.

A bonsai "feeling" is achieved by an aesthetic relationship of container to plant which is pleasing to the gardener-artist. The selection of the plants and the shaping or "sculpturing" of the material used will be a matter of one's creativity and personal taste. Pseudo-bonsai is free of the classic Japanese rules; but you should keep them in mind as they relate to the total effect. Your plant material can be as untraditional to the art as you wish. You may use a seedling plant just the right shape for the effect you want; or you may locate a root-bound plant at a nursery that will lend itself to instant bonsai with a little pruning and the right container.

You might even choose a succulent —the easy jade plant, an ice plant, an oxalis, a geranium or a coleus.

When using such material as succulents and coleus, you are not actually dwarfing a plant in this instant bonsai procedure—merely creating a mood.

Your plant will eventually need to be repotted, and most probably will require frequent but easy pruning to maintain its bonsai feeling. Some of the succulent material will not require repotting so much as pinching off new growth as it appears. Other plants, like the coleus, will outgrow their bonsai life. You will then make cuttings and start again with a fresh plant to create another bonsai mood.

Pseudo-bonsai, of course, requires good horticultural practices—watering and feeding according to the kind of plant you are growing.

73

The silvery Dud- a succulent collec-
leyas (D. subrigida tion of this con-
and D. brittonia) tainer garden.
take center stage in

These succulents, uality in a vertical
'Hens-and-Chick- Pagoda Planter.
ens' (Sempervivum),
show their individ-

Succulents-their relatives and friends

The fascinating world of succulents is a wide, wide
world of astounding variety. All cacti are succulents; but
not all succulents are cacti. Succulents include all of
the cactus family—both tropical and desert species; many
are in the lily family; some are cousins of the daisy,
while still others are part of the bromeliad clan.

Succulents are the camels of the plant kingdom; for
like the camel they devised some very clever survival
techniques for conserving water to carry them through
periods of drought. Some learned the art of disguise, and
imitated stones, to avoid being eaten by animals.

Not all are arid area types, such as the desert cacti.
Some are from tropical areas where there are long dry
seasons followed by a short season of heavy rains, but with
moist air and dry terrain following the rainy period. These
areas gave birth to the tropical cacti such as *Rhipsalis*
and *Epiphyllum* or "Orchid cactus." The lily family includes
such succulent members as the well known Aloes
(A. Vera being popular as a skin treatment for burns); the
"Elephant foot palm or Pony tail Palm" from Mexico—
Beaucarnea recurvata, and the many Sansevieria (Mother-
in-law's tongue). These are but a few that belong to
a succulent world of thousands.

Basics for container growing

Succulents make interesting and relatively easy-to-grow
container plants. For us to generalize too much can be
dangerous; but with a word of caution, to observe your
plants for indications of their individual preferences,
you should have good success with succulents, if these
few basic suggestions are followed:

Choosing a container. Uppermost in importance when
selecting the container is DRAINAGE. A clay pot just large
enough to accommodate the plant without overcrowding
its roots is the container of choice for most succulents.
If a small plant is placed in a pot that is too large, the water
cannot be taken up by the plant fast enough and rot may
occur. Bonsai containers are such versatile favorites.
They do a splendid job of show-casing succulents, and their
drainage holes are ideal. Use a fiberglass windowscreen
mesh (obtainable in hardware stores or garden centers)
to cover holes so your potting soil won't spill through.

Most succulents require drying between waterings.
That is another reason for preference of a clay pot rather
than plastic or other non-porous material. In a clay or other
porous material, it's easier to control the wet-dry needs of
your succulents. This is not to say, however, "Never plant a
succulent in a plastic pot." In a plastic container, you

This is instant staging of succulents adding charm to a patio. Oscularia deltoides, *lower left, with assorted* Crassulaceae.

One collector's originality combines ceramic and garden art using 'Medusa's head' (Euphorbia caput-medusae).

needn't water as often, and it's good for "vacationing" your plant while you're away. It won't dry out as fast.

Watering. Succulents, like any other plant, prefer rain water or bottled water. Quality of the water is important. Remember that succulents, like other kinds of plants, are sensitive to salt which is high in the water in certain areas; also high in softened water. Accumulated salts in root area cripple growth, cause eventual death. About every fourth watering, in order to leach (flush) accumulated salts from the root area, fill pot with water from top, let drain and repeat 3 times.

During their growing season, they should be watered whenever the soil has begun to dry out; but during their period of rest, always hold back on watering. Most succulents are sensitive to being wet when the weather is cold. In late fall when the temperatures begin to drop, dole out the water, allowing just enough to keep the roots alive. A turkey baster is handy for fall or winter watering when just a sip or two is allowed—just enough to maintain the roots and avoid wilting. Sometimes, for days at a stretch in winter, misting the surface of the soil and wetting the outside of the pot (using an ordinary plastic spray bottle) is all that's necessary.

Don't allow foliage to get limp and shriveled before watering. Learn to observe your plants, because they can tell you when they want water or when they want to rest. Not all of your succulents will want to be watered as frequently as some others. Not all will want to rest as early or for as long as others. By watching closely, getting to know them better and understanding their responses, your reaction to their needs will become automatic.

When night temperatures begin to rise, and when the plant begins to show signs of fresh growth, it's time to begin normal, thorough watering again. Set the pots in a pan of water and allow them to "drink" until the soil is just moist on top.

Potting Soil. Succulents need an open, well-draining mix. Although they are all—including the desert cacti— touted as "requiring" a lean (low nutritive content) mix, experienced specialists agree that a fairly rich soil mix is actually preferred by most succulent plants in cultivation. Most tropical succulents (see Selection Guide, page 79) prefer an acid condition, while others—arid region species—like a slight alkalinity. This acid-alkalinity factor may be controlled by soil additives. See Container Soils, page 8.

Fertilizing. Fertilizing succulents should be done *during the growing period only.* Never fertilize with more than a fourth to a third of the recommended dilution printed on the package directions. It is always better to feed a little

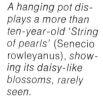

A large clay bowl container supports three others in diminishing size to form a terraced collection of *Crassulaceae.*

A hanging pot displays a more than ten-year-old 'String of pearls' (Senecio rowleyanus), *showing its daisy-like blossoms, rarely seen.*

Ceramic basket contains Aichryson dichotomum *from the Canary Islands with its spoon shaped green leaves and yellow flowers.*

and often—about every third watering. Stop all feeding as soon as the plants quit showing further seasonal growth. Never feed during their resting period. It would be about as welcome as a plate of food forced on you while trying to sleep.

Air temperature and light. *Good Air Circulation* is very important to the health of your succulents. Stagnant air encourages mealybugs on any "dry growing" plant. Early morning humidity is actually welcomed by all—even your desert cacti—but it is equally important that evaporation take place to remove any excess moisture within a short period. Example, the morning dew (the only moisture some receive for months at a time in their native habitat) that freshens foliage and disappears with the warming rays of the morning sun. Don't allow your succulents to go to bed with their leaves wet. Keep them cool (not cold) at night, let the full sun warm them during the day (unless they're the kind that prefer filtered sun, such as the tropical cacti) and they'll respond to your tender loving care like the show-offs they can be.

Few succulents tolerate frost. Plan to give them winter protection with as much sunlight as possible.

Succulents as shade plants can do remarkable things. Like the ice plant, which makes a fine green hanging basket. True ice plant—"mesembs" *(mesembryanthemum)* of the aizoaceae family—always has an "icy" appearance, as if moisture were formed on a container of frozen

material. If it doesn't have that kind of "beaded" look, it's not true ice plant.

Some succulents get more color in sun; others show nothing but green, no matter what degree of light they get. Most tend to change their leaf size, becoming more compact in habit and much smaller with more sun and stress; conversely they become larger, less compact and more lush with more shading, water and nutrient.

Guide to selecting succulents

Over 9000 plants are recognized in the extremely diverse group called "Succulents." The name is an arbitrary one which applies to many different plant families, including Cacti, and all having the ability to withstand varying degrees of drought. The task of cataloging, even those most desirable and practical for the home garden is overwhelming.

The guide, page 79, does not attempt to list nor to advise in the selection of *very rare* succulents or those of *difficult culture.* There are many specialty nurseries, that list plants for the collector—the rare and not-so-rare; the easy and not-so-easy of culture.

This list used botanical latin nomenclature. This avoids mistaken identity, the frustration of receiving the wrong plant when ordering or seeking additional information on a specific plant. Common names vary throughout the

'Ghost plant'
(Graptopetalum
paraguayense)
*becomes the brim
of an Easter
bonnet on this
ceramic lady's
head.*

'Donkey's tail'
(Sedum morganianum)
*festoons from
pots beneath pro-
tective branches,
adding lushness to
this cool scene.*

*This garden foun-
tain lends a touch
of formality with
clay baskets
centered with
Echeveria elegans
circled by Senecio
repens.*

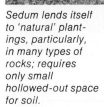

*Sedum lends itself
to 'natural' plant-
ings, particularly,
in many types of
rocks; requires
only small
hollowed-out space
for soil.*

*Sedum pachyphyllum
reaches for the
overhead light
displaying it as a
graceful upright.*

*Flowers are not
necessary for color
with* Echeveria
hybrid 'Meridian.'

Hung to receive filtered light, the cascading blossoms of Epiphyllum 'Duchess Kaiserine' hybrid *are a striking display.*

An infinite variety of form and color are offered as in this nursery assortment of succulents.

Hybrid Christmas cacti (Zygocactus 'Kris Kringle' *and white Z. truncatus delicatus) are free flowering even when small.*

The flower of Echtinopsis 'Gates hybrid' *makes this cactus a worthwhile addition to the container sun garden.*

Bright blossoms just beginning to crown the geometric pattern of Mammillaria pseudoperbella.

country, and the same name is often used for many diverse kinds of plants. Where a common name is in general usage we show it in quotes following the botanical name. Perhaps not all your friends have such easy names as John Jones or Jim Smith. Plants, like the rest of your friends, have names—sometimes strange sounding. Learning their names will pay dividends when shopping for plants or checking on their culture.

Because succulents are not one family, but comprise members of so many diverse families, these recommendations only seek to open the door to a world of fascinating color, form and texture. These are the plants more generally available and of easy culture. They are especially adaptable to container gardening. Some are suitable to display in floor containers; many do well in hanging baskets. Try a group of three or more that display color contrasts as well as varied textures. The cactus group usually available in general nurseries are slow growing and will not be in a hurry to graduate to larger pots.

Try the tiny Mesembryanthemum oscularia with its fragrant purple-pink flowers and heady perfume as a ground cover, in a hanging basket or a potted tropical for contrast in color. (An interesting foil for a rubber plant, dumb cane, etc.) Let your own taste and imagination be your guide. The avant gardener should not be timid about trying something new as long as it is within the bounds of sound culture.

A guide to the succulent family

Family	Genus	Species	Variety Or Common Name	Code
Aizoaceae	Faucaria	tigrina	'Tiger Jaw'	PT-AR
		speciosa	'Tiger Jaw'	PT-AR
		tuberculosa	——	PT-AR
	Fenestraria	aurantiaca	——	PT-AR
		rhopalophylla	'Baby Toes'	PT-AR
	Lithops	(Note 1)	'Living Rocks'	PT-AR
	Mesembryanthemum	oscularia	'Ice Plant'	HC-FR-AR
Asclepiadaceae	Ceropegia	woodii	'Rosary Vine'	HC-TR
			'String of Hearts'	HC-TR
	Hoya	bella	——	HC-TR-FR
		carnosa	'Wax Plant'	HC-TR-FR
		c.	'Vatiegata'	HC-TR-FR
		c.	'Tricolor'	HC-TR-FR
		c.	'Compacta'	HC-TR-FR
	Stapelia	(Note 1)	'Starfish Flower'	PT-HC-TR
Cactaceae (Cacti)	Astrophytum	asterias	'Sea Urchin Cactus'	PT
		(Note 1)		
	Cephalocereus	senilis	'Old Man Cactus'	PT
	Echinopsis	(Note 1)	——	SFF
		multiplex	'Easter Lily Cactus'	SFF
	Epiphyllum	(Note 1)	'Orchid Cactus'	HC-FR-TR
	Schlumbergera	bridgesii	'Christmas Cactus'	HC-TR
		gaertneri	'Easter Cactus'	HC-TR
	Zygocactus	truncatus	'Thanksgiving Cactus'	HC-TR
	Lobivia	(Note 1)	——	PT-SFF-AR
	Mammillaria	(Note 1)	——	PT-SFF-AR
	Notocactus	(Note 1)	——	PT-SFF-AR
	Rebutia	(Note 1)	——	PT-SFF-AR
	Rhipsalis	(Note 1)	——	HC-TR
Compositae (Daisy relatives)	Senecio	rowleyanus	'String of Pearls'	HC-TR/AR
		mikanoides	'German Ivy'	HC-TR/AR
Crassulaceae	Aeoneum	balsamiferum	——	PT-FR-TR/AR
		arboreum	atropurpureum	PT-TR/AR
			a. 'Schwarzkopf'	PT-TR/AR
		decorum	——	DSM-PT-TR/AR
		haworthii	'Pin Wheel'	PT-TR/AR
		pseudotabulaeforme	plain	DSM-PT-TR/AR
			crested	DSM-PT-TR/AR
	Crassula	argentea	'arborescens' or 'Jade Plant'	PT-PF-TR/AR
			'Sunset'	PT-PF-TR/AR
			hybrid portulacea	PT-PF-TR/AR
		cooperi	——	HC-PT-DSM-TR/AR
		falcata	'Rhocea' or 'Scarlet Paintbrush'	PT-PF-FR-TR/AR
		schmidtii	'Necklace Vine'	DSM-HC-PT-TR/AR
	Echeveria	agavoides	——	PT-TR/AR
		glauca	——	PT-TR/AR
		perfossa	——	HC-TR/AR
	Kalanchoe	tomentosa	'Panda Plant'	PT-TR/AR
			'Vivid'	PT-PF-TR/AR
		beharensis	'Felt Plant'	PT-PF-TR/AR
		pumila	——	PT-HC-TR/AR
	Sedum	dasyphyllum	——	DSM-HC-TR/AR
		morganianum	'Burro Tail' or 'Donkey Tail'	HC-TR/AR
		multiceps	'Miniature Joshua' (deciduous)	DSM-TR/AR
		weinbergii	'Ghost Plant'	HC-PT-TR/AR
	Sempervivum	tectorum	'Hen-and-Chicken'	PT-TR/AR
		(Note 1)		
Cycadaceae (cycads)	Cycas	revoluta	'Sago Palm'	PF-TR
Euphrbiaceae (Ephorbia)	Euphorbia	splendens	'Crown of Thorns'	PT-PF-TR/AR
		caput medusae	'Medusa's Head'	PT-HC-TR/AR
		obesa		PT-TR/AR
		pulcherrima	'Poinsettia'	PT-PF-TR/AR
Lillaceae (Lily)	Aloe	aristata	——	DSM-PT-TR/AR
		rauhii	——	DSM-PT-TR/AR
		vera	'Medicine Plant'	PT-TR/AR
	Haworthia	fasciata	——	PT-TR/AR
		glabrata	——	PT-TR/AR
		margaritifera	'Margaritifera'	DSM-PT-TR/AR
		turgida	'Palida'	PT-TR/AR
		setata	'Lace Haworthia'	DSM-PT-TR/AR
	Boweia	volubilis (deciduous)	'False Sea Onion'	DSM-PT-TR/AR
	Beaucarnea	recurvata	'Ponytail'	PT-PF-TR/AR
Oxalidaceae	Oxalis	peduncularis	——	DSM-PT-TR/AR

Note 1 — Any of this genus that are available in a general nursery or garden center are recommended.
Code: **DSM**=dwarf to small • **HC**=suitable for hanging container • **PT**=pot specimen for table display • **PF**=pot specimen for floor display • **SFF**=spiny but free-flowering • **FR**=fragrance • **TR**=tropical—likes acid soil, more moisture • **AR**=arid—likes slightly alkaline soil • **TR/AR**=intermediate.

Vegetables in containers

In our early experiments in growing vegetables in containers we tried to determine the minimum size container required for the various vegetables. It was evident that the size of the root space in a container was no handicap to plant growth if the proper nutrients and moisture were always available. The trouble we had with the minimum sized container was in keeping the plant supplied with water as the plant matured. The growth and fruit set of large-fruited tomato in a 6″ pot was amazing but we found ourselves watering twice a day or more frequently. Eventually the small container is filled with roots, with little or no reservoir for moisture.

From our experience the minimum size container in which a vegetable variety can be grown is not always the practical size. In recommending container size for the various vegetables, we have tried to keep in mind the *practical* minimum size.

We have used all sizes of pots, cans, plastic buckets, plastic trash containers, garbage cans, bulb pots, azalea pots, fiber pots, paint buckets, half whiskey barrels, and fruit baskets—peck and bushel.

The larger the container, the larger volume of soil. With a large volume of soil, plant roots can draw on a reserve of moisture and nutrients. Watering and feeding is less a chore than when the plants are confined in small containers. But it doesn't make sense to give a plant a soil depth of 16″ or 18″ if it can produce in a container 6″ to 8″ deep.

When gardening on a balcony or roof, the weight of the container must be considered. To get 50 square feet of planting space with 16″ deep containers calls for 67 cubic feet of soil mix. If the containers or boxes are 8″ deep, only half that amount of soil would be needed.

Size and gallonage

There is no such thing as a standard size container except in the old clay pots which graduate uniformly from 2″ to 16″.

A gallon size container is described by different manufacturers as 7¼″x6¼″, 7½″x7½″, and 6¼″x7″. The dimensions are diameter by depth. The thickness of the material—fiber, metal, type of plastic—and the *taper* of the pot accounts for the difference of the dimensions.

Sizes of containers by gallons:
1 gallon—7¼″x6¼″
2 gallon—8″x8″
3 gallon—10″x10″
4 gallon—12″x11″
5 gallon—12″x12″
6 gallon—13″x13″

Sizes of standard redwood octagonal planter tubs:
12″x11″
14″x12½″
16″x14″
18″x15″

A productive container garden

With substantial production of vegetables for the kitchen in mind, we worked out the following patio or balcony garden as a sample of the possible crop yield from containers.

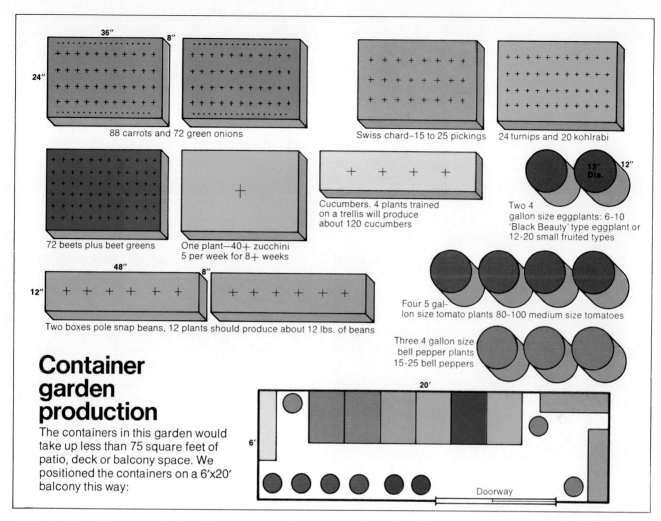

88 carrots and 72 green onions

Swiss chard—15 to 25 pickings

24 turnips and 20 kohlrabi

72 beets plus beet greens

One plant—40+ zucchini 5 per week for 8+ weeks

Cucumbers. 4 plants trained on a trellis will produce about 120 cucumbers

Two 4 gallon size eggplants: 6-10 'Black Beauty' type eggplant or 12-20 small fruited types

Two boxes pole snap beans, 12 plants should produce about 12 lbs. of beans

Four 5 gallon size tomato plants 80-100 medium size tomatoes

Three 4 gallon size bell pepper plants 15-25 bell peppers

Doorway

Container garden production

The containers in this garden would take up less than 75 square feet of patio, deck or balcony space. We positioned the containers on a 6'x20' balcony this way:

After a year of experimenting we settled on three types of containers:

For onions, carrots, beets, turnips, kohlrabi, and zucchini, we used boxes 24"x36" and 8" deep.

For pole beans, cucumbers, tomatoes, and peas, a narrow long box, 12"x48" and 8" deep, was built with a trellis for training these vegetables vertically.

For peppers, eggplant, and tomatoes, we used single 4 and 5 gallon sized containers.

Typical plantings in the 24"x36" inch box; 4 rows of carrots, 5" apart, thinned to 3" apart in the row. Also 2 rows of onion sets for green onions, set 2" apart in the row. See notes on these vegetables in the following individual vegetable list and in the illustration above.

When you grow vegetables in containers you can take advantage of the various little climates around the house and garden. You might give the heat loving eggplant a spot where it gets not only full sunlight but the reflected heat off a south wall.

Because of the emphasis placed on the need to locate the vegetable plot in a location receiving full sunlight, many gardeners assume that all vegetables require full sunlight.

The truth is that many vegetables will tolerate filtered shade. In the 12-page Home and Garden Bulletin No. 163, the USDA tabulates the light requirements of various vegetables. In the following discussion of vegetables, we allow the bulletin to be our authority on light requirements. (We have grown tomatoes in locations where we knew they would not get enough sun for a normal crop. We were thankful for half a crop.)

In recommending the size of the containers we indicate whether it's the 24"x36" box or the 12"x48" box or a 2, 3, 4, or 5 gallon container. Whether the boxes you use vary from those dimensions is not important. We use those dimensions to indicate whether a wide or narrow box is the more efficient.

The vegetables

Beets

Season: Cool, early and late.

Light: Tolerate partial shade.

Spacing: 2" to 3" apart in row.

Container: 24"x36"x8" box.

Harvest: When 1" to 2" in diameter.

Comments: Thin plants when 6" to 8" high. Use thinnings for greens. Our favorite varieties: 'Golden Beet' (55 days) "Tops taste better than spinach when boiled as greens." 'Detroit Dark Red' (60 days), round shape.

Carrots

Season: Spring, early summer, fall.

Light: Tolerate partial shade.

Spacing: 1½" to 3" in the row. Thin early to avoid tangled roots.

Container: 24"x36"x10" box.

Harvest: For small carrots, when ½" to 1" in diameter.

Comments: Plant for succession. Choose short rooted varieties, such as 'Nantes Half Long' (70 days), cylin-

Beets yield two crops —first the thinnings or "greens," then the mature harvest.

Romaine lettuce with its upright growth, can be close-planted in containers.

Recycled tire serves as small raised bed.

Leaf lettuce in variety makes a colorful hanging basket.

drical roots 6"-7" long. 'Royal Chantenay' (70 days), broad shouldered, roots 4-7 inches.

Chives

Season: A hardy perennial.

Light: Grow in partial shade, as in a kitchen window.

Spacing: 2" to 3" (in clusters).

Container: 4" pots.

Harvest: Clip as needed. If not clipped, chives produce attractive lavender flower heads.

Comments: For a quick harvest, buy plants. Small clumps spread rapidly. Chives should be divided occasionally so they do not get too thick.

Cucumbers

Season: Warm summer.

Light: Require full sunlight.

Spacing: 12" to 16" in 48" box.

Container: 12"x48"x8" box with trellis.

Harvest: Pick before hard seeds form.

Comments: Many, many varieties. Train the strong vining types on a trellis. One plant will produce 20 to 30 fruits. The bush type, such as 'Patio Pik' and 'Salty' produce on vines only 18" to 24" long.

Eggplant

Season: Warm summer.

Light: Needs full sunlight.

Spacing: One plant to a container.

Container: 4 to 5 gallon size.

Harvest: At any stage from ⅓ to ⅔ their normal mature size. Good fruit has a high gloss.

Comments: Choose early varieties such as 'Mission Bell' in short-season areas. Standard varieties require high heat and long growing season. In containers, the varieties with medium to small-sized fruits carried high on the plant are more interesting than the lower growing heavy-fruited varieties.

Kale

Season: Grows best in cool days of fall. Flavor improved by frost.

Light: Tolerates partial shade.

Spacing: 6".

Container: Plant in 12"x48" box.

Harvest: When tall enough for greens; cut whole plants or take larger leaves.

Comments: Grows to 12" to 18" tall and as wide. The leaves of the variety 'Blue Curled Scotch' are as curled as parsley.

The Ball Company, supplier to bedding plant growers, demonstrates productivity of tomatoes, eggplant, peppers and cucumbers grown in Jiffy-tubs.

Leeks

Season: Winter hardy. 130 to 150 days from seed. 80 to 90 days from transplants.

Light: Tolerate partial shade.

Spacing: 2″ to 3″ in the row.

Container: Grow in 24″x36″ box.

Harvest: When 1″ in diameter and white part is 5″ to 6″ long.

Comments: Leeks do not bulb as onions do. The thickened stems can be blanched by hilling soil around them.

Lettuce

Season: Early spring or fall.

Light: Tolerates partial shade.

Spacing: Leaf lettuce 4″ to 6″. Head lettuce 10″.

Container: Head lettuce: Give it room—space 10″ apart in the row. Use 24″x36″ box, or 12″x48″ box.
Leaf lettuce: Any container will do. Can be harvested as it grows, leaf by leaf.

Comments: High temperatures and long days cause lettuce to flower (bolt). For all but early spring and fall plantings, choose varieties that are slow to bolt, such as 'Summer Bibb,' 'Buttercrunch,' 'Oakleaf,' and 'Slobolt.'

Onions (green)

Season: Sets in early spring and in September.

Light: Green onions grow in partial shade, mature bulbs need full sun.

Spacing: 2″ in the row.

Container: Any container 6″ or more deep.

Harvest: When 8″ to 10″ tall.

Comments: Leave one green onion every 4 inches or so to form a bulb. The small bulbs are usable as cooked onions after they dry out.

Parsley

Season: Cool. A biennial—producing foliage the first year, going to seed the next spring. Treat as an annual.

Light: Does well in partial shade. Will grow on kitchen windowsills.

Spacing: 6″ to 8″ in the row in box.

Container: 4″ pot indoors.

Harvest: Clip for garnish.

Comments: For garnishing, the variety 'Moss Curled,' also called 'Extra Curled Dwarf,' is the standard curled leaf variety. For flavoring, the ''plain'' or ''single'' is the standard variety. The 'Hamburg Rooted' is grown for its parsnip-like roots 6″ or longer and about 2″ thick at the neck.

Above: Potato harvest from peck fruit baskets was fair, but next year we will use bushel baskets.

Below: In this old-tire, high-rise planting, potatoes were planted at ground level and then progressively "hilled-up," tire by tire, as the vines grew.

Where space is limited, a collection of containers make a fair vegetable "patch."

Peppers

Season: Warm summer.

Light: Require full sunlight.

Spacing: 14" to 18" apart in row in a box.

Container: Allow one plant per 2 to 4 gallon container.

Harvest: Harvest bell peppers when 2" to 3" in diameter.

Comments: When August rolls around our favorite vegetables in containers are peppers. Almost any variety, hot or sweet, has ornamental values worth displaying on patio or deck—shiny green leaves, small white flowers, fruits in many shapes and colors, green, yellow, red.

Potatoes

Season: Late spring, early summer.

Light: Require full sunlight.

Spacing: 2 seed pieces to the container.

Container: 5 gallon size or larger.

Harvest: When tops die down.

Comments: Plant seed pieces ¾ the way down in the container, adding a mulch type soil as the potatoes grow, so potatoes can be "picked" rather than dug.

Swiss Chard

Season: Spring, summer, fall.

Light: Tolerates partial shade.

Spacing: 4" to 5" in the row; 6" between rows.

Container: Any container 6" to 8" deep.

Harvest: When leaves are 3" or more in length.

Comments: Only one planting is needed. Outer leaves may be harvested without injury to the plant. A great "cut and come again" plant.

Tomato

Season: Poor fruit set when night temperatures are below 60° or above 75°. Needs 3 to 4 months of temperatures in the 65° to 85° range.

Raised beds filled with a good soil mix increase crop yields and the joy of gardening.

Light: Requires full sunlight at least 6 hours a day.

Spacing: Depends on variety and how trained.

Container: Give the strong, large-fruited varieties a 4 to 5 gallon sized container. See below for sizes of "container" varieties.

Comments: There are hundreds of varieties. Check your nurseryman or Extension Agent for varieties adapted to your area. A number of varieties especially suited for container growing have been introduced in the last few years. If you are using garden soil or compost in your soil mix, you should favor the disease resistant varieties. Resistance is indicated by the initials "V"—Verticillium; "F"—Fusarium; "N"—Nematode. (Container gardeners using sterilized soil mixes of peat moss and vermiculite or perlite avoid soil-borne diseases. See page 8.)

Container tomatoes. 'Tiny Tim' *(55 days from transplant).* The midget of the group. Only 15″ tall with ¾″ scarlet fruit. Give it a 6″ pot or hanging basket, or plant 2 in an 8″ pot.

'Small Fry' VF *(55 days).* Vigorous grower to 30″ bearing 1″ fruits in profusion. Best in a 12″ pot or box with trellis. Beautiful in a hanging basket.

'Atom' *(60 days).* Similar to 'Small Fry' in growth habit. Heavy production of small 1″ fruits. Well adapted to indoor growing in 8″ to 10″ pots, or hanging baskets.

Burpee's 'Pixie Hybrid' *(55 days).* Grows 14″ to 18″ tall. Fruits 1¾″. Grow in 8″ pot or hanging basket. Will produce indoors in winter in sunny window.

'Patio Hybrid' F *(70 days).* Extra sturdy, main stem is like the trunk of a small tree. Grows to about 30″. Needs no staking until heavy with its 2″ fruit. Best in a 12″ tub or pot.

'Stakeless' F *(78 days).* Similar to "Patio" in sturdy growth habit. Dense foliage. Grows 20″ to 24″ tall with 5 to 8-ounce (2″ and larger) fruits. Plant in a 10″ to 12″ pot.

'Tumblin' Tom' VFN *(48 days).* A new introduction in the hanging basket class. Heavy yield of 1½″ to 2″ fruits. Vine grows 20″ to 24″ tall.

'Small Fry' is a big producer of good-eating, inch-size tomatoes.

Here, staked in a tub the 'Atom' tomato performs handsomely.

'Tumblin' Tom' is a heavy producer in tubs or hanging baskets.

Trellis attached to planter box supports the vigorous growth and generous production of 'Small Fry.'

Burpee's 'Early Salad Hybrid' *(45 days)*. Compact plants grow only 6″ to 8″ high with a spread of about 2′. One plant will produce from 250 to 300 fruits measuring 1½″ to 1¾″.

'Presto' *(60 days)*. The small-leaved, rather open vine grows to about 2′ tall with heavy yield of half-dollar size fruits. Grow in a 3 to 5 gallon container and give it the support of a short stake.

Turnips

Season: Cool. Plant 4 to 6 weeks before last frost in spring and 6 to 8 weeks before first fall freeze.

Light: Tolerate partial shade.

Spacing: Thin when large enough to make greens and leave others to mature.

Container: We combine them with kohlrabi in 24″x36″ box, and harvest both when small.

Comments: We are partial to 'Tokyo Cross' variety, but all varieties are good when picked small.

Zucchini

Season: Warm summer.

Light: Does best in full sunlight.

Spacing: One plant per 5 gallon container.

Container: Larger than 12″ in diameter. We used the 24″x36″ box.

Harvest: When 1½″ to 2″ in diameter.

Comments: One plant will produce 6 or more fruits a week.

The larger the size of the container, the greater the production of strawberries.

There's more

The list of vegetables, fruits, and herbs that will thrive in containers or hanging baskets is almost without limits. Grapes, figs, dwarf peaches and nectarines, dwarf cherries, plums, and apricots, are all container subjects. Probably most rewarding in containers, large and small, is the strawberry.

Strawberries

After growing strawberries in the ground, in hanging baskets, in clay and wood strawberry barrels, in 5-gallon plastic pails, in planter boxes, and in vertical walls, we can't say that any one way is "best."

For maximum production the container should be large enough to nourish a root system that's at least 8" wide and 8" deep. In the field, the top foot of soil is filled with roots. Just beneath the surface, horizontal roots extend a foot or more on all sides of the base of the plant. Water is drawn chiefly from 6" to 12". Restriction of the root system in too small a container reduces production. Reduction of any part of the root system effects the whole plant.

It may be that the production of 2 crowded plants is as great as 1 plant with adequate root space, but this year we are planting only 4 plants to the 48" long planter box. We think that we will get more berries over a longer time than if we planted 8 crowns.

Herbs

A box 12"x48"x8" deep will serve well as a patio herb garden. Chives, garden thyme, basil, marjoram, and summer savory will do well in the confines of this planter box. The sprawling growth habit of the various mints and oregano suggest their use in hanging baskets.
If you have room for 12" pots or tubs, you can add these to your herb list: tarragon ,winter savory, rosemary, and a young Sweet Bay tree.

"Spaghetti sauce" hanging basket supports marjoram, thyme, garlic, chives and basil.

*Above: An old step-ladder used as a garden display stand. When vine crops are grown vertically, the steps make excellent "resting places" for heavy fruits such as melon and squash.
Right: A melon, supported by a small shelf, takes its weight off the vine.*

Below: Pantyhose or old nylon stockings can be used as slings to support melons growing up a fence.

A wall becomes a flower bed in this patio where other gardening space is limited.

The vertical dimension

Gardeners, frustrated by limited floor level space for growing plants, have been forced into the vertical dimension. They have made use of vertical space in many ways—some new and some old as the hills.

Throughout the world, wherever container gardening has flourished, gardeners have looked upon all smooth vertical surfaces as gardening areas. A 6-foot high fence, 20-feet long, adds 120 square feet to a small garden.

Many a gardener has disregarded the advice of those who claim that "vine crops such as melons, cucumbers, squash, and others which require considerable space, may not be advisable in the small garden." The small space gardeners go on the assumption that any vine that spreads wide can be trained to grow tall.

The melon and squash may be too heavy for the vertically grown vine, but a few short shelves on a fence as resting places for melons or large squash will take the weight off the vines.

Planter boxes of wood in various dimensions are most effective when arranged on an existing fence. Support planters with brackets or shelves for quick changes in the display. Square-sided half-baskets of wire are available for use as a sphagnum moss basket against a fence or wall.

Checkerboard fence

Small space gardeners have made use of the fence in other ways. By making slight changes in the construction of a fence panel, it can be converted into a checkerboard planter and display area. Use 4"x6" posts in the section to be planted. Cover the back of the fence with regular fencing material (1"x6" or 1"x8" boards). Use 2"x6"s for the verticals and cross pieces between the posts. We have planted this type of a fence using 4"x4" posts and a grid of 2"x4"s, but find that the 2"x4"s give too shallow a width for easy maintenance.

Staple wire mesh in the area to be planted. (A welded wire with a 2"x2" or 2"x2½" mesh is ideal.) Use wood facing strips to cover the edges of wire. Starting from the bottom of the wire, work in a layer of sphagnum moss, ½" to 1" thick. Leave open space at top of wire until soil has been added. Fill with lightweight planter mix up to top mesh. Finish filling with straight sphagnum moss.

Free standing vertical wall

Looking at this vertical planting scheme, the space hungry gardeners ask themselves why not use all the fence as a planting area. The vertical garden wall that has been popularized in Europe calls for special construction details. When the wire mesh is used in large areas, it will bulge out unless held by inside wire braces. In a wall 6 feet high, the problem of the filler-mix settling too much is solved by installing one or two wire mesh partitions.

We have built (and used for two years) a simplified European wall planter using black plastic film instead of wire and sphagnum moss.

Our box, 8" wide, 34" long, and 44" deep, was to be a free standing affair in front of an 8' high hedge. The end pieces of 2"x8" rough redwood were cut 6' long to serve as posts and inserted in the ground when the box was complete. Ends were cross braced with 2"x2"s at top and bottom. Exterior plywood was used for the back and bottom of the box. Drainage holes were drilled in the bottom plywood. The black plastic film for the front of the box was secured by a grid of 1"x2"s on 6" centers.

The 1"x2"s hold the plastic and the planter mix behind it. When inserting plants, work in some damp sphagnum moss to plug the hole in the plastic.

One square before planting

Plant by inserting root ball through the wire

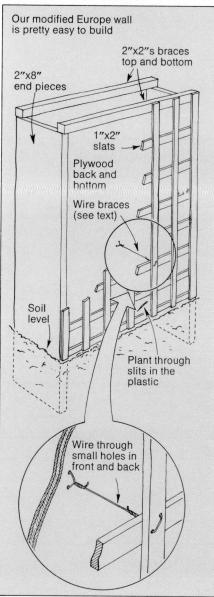

Our modified Europe wall is pretty easy to build

2"x2"s braces top and bottom

2"x8" end pieces

1"x2" slats

Plywood back and bottom

Wire braces (see text)

Soil level

Plant through slits in the plastic

Wire through small holes in front and back

Above: two versions of the checkerboard fence.

Above: the vertical strawberry walls when first planted. Below: two years later.

Above: in early spring, roll-around box planted with lettuce. Below: in summer, same box—planted with fibrous begonias, impatiens and coleus—moved to partially shady area.

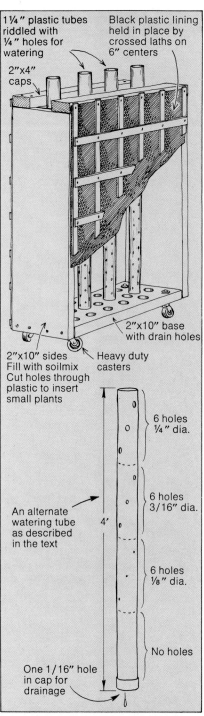

1¼" plastic tubes riddled with ¼" holes for watering

Black plastic lining held in place by crossed laths on 6" centers

2"x4" caps

2"x10" base with drain holes

2"x10" sides Fill with soilmix Cut holes through plastic to insert small plants

Heavy duty casters

An alternate watering tube as described in the text

4'

6 holes ¼" dia.

6 holes 3/16" dia.

6 holes ⅛" dia.

No holes

One 1/16" hole in cap for drainage

Build and plant your living pillar on the ground or work bench then stand it up for display. See text

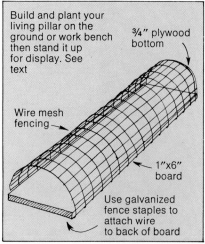

¾" plywood bottom

Wire mesh fencing

1"x6" board

Use galvanized fence staples to attach wire to back of board

Roll-around wall

The free standing vertical box can be planted on both sides. If planted on both sides, the box should be wider—at least 10". We attached wheels to our planter so that we could move it to get the light—sun or part shade— we wanted.

Our roll around is about to enter its third year of service. Early in the season there's lettuce on one side and pansies on the other. Through the summer months, the roll around gets a place on a shady patio and it bulges with impatiens, front and back.

To make sure that the soil mix is evenly watered, 1¼" plastic pipes were placed 6" apart in the box as the soil was added. The sections of pipe were capped at the bottom and holes were drilled for even watering.

In the boxes we have built we have riddled the pipe with ¼" holes. By watering the top soil to take care of the first 2' of soil and using the pipes to water the lower 2', we have had two years of successful plantings. However, a gardener who watered only through the pipes pointed out that we were passing out inaccurate instructions. If only the pipes are used for watering, follow this good gardener's instructions:

a) We drilled no holes below a foot from the bottom except for a 1/16 hole in the cap to allow the pipe to drain slowly after watering.
b) In the 2nd foot above the bottom we drilled 6 holes 1/8" in diameter.
c) In the 3rd foot up we drilled 6 holes 3/16" in diameter.
d) In the top foot we drilled 6 holes ¼" in diameter. The graduation in the hole size was made to compensate for the difference in water "head" between the top and bottom.

Living pillars

If you like the idea of vertical planting but consider the wall garden or the roll-around too complex a project, the construction of the flowering pillar is more simple. You'll need a piece of 1"x6" redwood or cedar cut to the desired length, and welded wire with a 2"x2" or 2"x2½" mesh. A 14" length of wire will form a half circle when bent and stapled to the board. Use exterior grade plywood cut in a half circle, of the same dimensions as the half circle of wire, as a base for the pillar. Staple or nail edges of wire to back edge of board and plywood base. Work into the wire a half-inch of damp sphagnum moss. Fill the column with dampened, lightweight, planter mix. Plant in the same way as you would a hanging wire basket. See page 42.

Popular flowers for pillars are pansies or violas, or a combination of alyssum and violas, in early spring. We have used impatiens, fibrous begonias, and petunias.

When securing the pillar to a wall, protect the wall with a backing of roofing paper secured to the back board of the pillar.

We have used black plastic film instead of sphagnum moss to contain the planter mix.

To get a neat, wrinkle-free job with the plastic, cut the plastic about 2″ longer than the wire and 2″-3″ wider. Fold the extra 2″ of plastic over the top of the wire. Staple wire and plastic to one side of the board. Bend the wire in a half circle, guiding the overlapped plastic as you bend the wire. With the plastic smooth and straight against the wire, staple the wire and plastic to the other side of the board.

When filling the column with the mix, lean it forward so that the mix falls against the plastic.

We have made pillars using a 12″ wide backboard, both with wire and sphagnum moss, and with plastic. In the wire pillar we used strawberries and fibrous begonias. In the plastic lined pillar we planted 'Small Fry' tomatoes at the top and half way down.

The length of the pillar may be 4′, 8′, or anything in between.

Precautions. Before applying sphagnum moss, loosen it and moisten it evenly.

Planter mix should be watered in advance and poured into containers when damp. After first watering, the mix will settle. Add more mix.

Root ball of plants to be inserted through the sphagnum moss should be moist rather than wet. We water the 6 pack or flat about 3 hours before removing root ball.

Unless a timed-release fertilizer has been mixed into the planter mix, give the planter an application of diluted liquid fertilizer every third or fourth watering.

When watering, be sure the mix is moist from top to bottom. Add water until water drips from the bottom drainage holes.

Don't underestimate the weight of these large planters. The soil mix may be lightweight, but it holds a lot of water (weighing 8.3 pounds per gallon).

The original petunia "tree" was made with a half circle of 2″ mesh wire, stapled to a 1″x12″ board. A lining of sphagnum moss retains the planter mix. Petunia seedlings were inserted through the moss.

1″x12″ board

Hog wire with 2″ mesh

Planting mix

Sphagnum moss (or black plastic)

To line the wire with plastic follow all the steps outlined in the text.

Fold about 2″ of plastic over the wire

. . . and staple both to the back of the board.

Keep the plastic smooth against the wire as you bend it around and staple it to the other side of the board.

Pillar of spring bloom, planted horizontally, then raised to vertical wall position for special display.

Half cylinder strawberry pillar interplanted with impatiens for added color.

Kids and containers

The full story of our experiments with the green world and children of all ages is crammed into a book of 54 pages— A Child's Garden—A Guide for Parents and Teachers.

Books are available from Public Relations, Chevron Chemical Company, 200 Bush Street, San Francisco, CA 94104. The price is 50¢. Single copies free to teachers.

When the urge comes to plant a seed, let there be something to plant it in. The sculptor needs clay; the artist needs water colors, pencils, paints, canvas, brushes, etc.; the sign painter needs . . . ; the gardener needs dirt, soil, and a lot more. Think about these projects and the dozens more you would like to try. What materials will be needed? How many projects will be postponed because of the delay in collecting the necessary materials?

On these pages we present a visual don't-forget-list of the containers that might be used in the home or in the school. The teacher may scrounge, beg, borrow, or makedo with a wide variety of material, and at the same time buy garden supplies that make seed germination and the production of flowers, vegetables, shrubs and vines less a gamble.

There's plenty of "waste" material and a world of inexpensive items—not manufactured for the teacher's classroom—that belong in the experimenter's stockroom. Milk cartons in all sizes, egg cartons, aluminum pans and trays used in packaging and in the oven, plastic glasses, paper cups, etc.

Another group of materials is found in the *gardening aids* section of most seed catalogs, and in the larger garden centers. These are the products used by the commercial "bedding plant" growers. Many seed starting "kits" are collections based on materials used by professionals.

Lack of experience in "gardening" need be no hang-up when using this material. The teacher who is willing to follow directions becomes an "old pro" instantly.

Here are some of the items:

Synthetic soil mix: Jiffy Mix, Pro-Mix, Redi-Earth, Super Soil, First Step, etc. See page 16.

Jiffy-7 Pellets: A compressed peat pellet containing fertilizer. When placed in water it expands to make a 1¾ by 2-inch container. Seed is placed directly in container, before or after expanding.

Kys-Kube: A ready-to-use fiber cube containing fertilizer. Offered by many seed companies.

Fertl-Cubes: One-inch cubes made of a blend of mosses, plant food, perlite and vermiculite. Each cube has a small depression in which you can plant 2 or 3 seeds. Cubes always stay moist so seeds germinate quickly. Young seedlings are transplanted into Jiffy Pots or directly into the ground, without the usual setback.

Peat Pots—Fiber trays—strips: Containers made of peat or other fibrous material. Fill with synthetic soil mix for growing-on of seedlings. No root disturbance, as container with plant is set out in garden soil.

Plastic: Pots or trays in various sizes and shapes. *Must* have drain holes in the bottom. Filled with synthetic soil mix for growing seedlings. Root ball tipped out when transplanting.

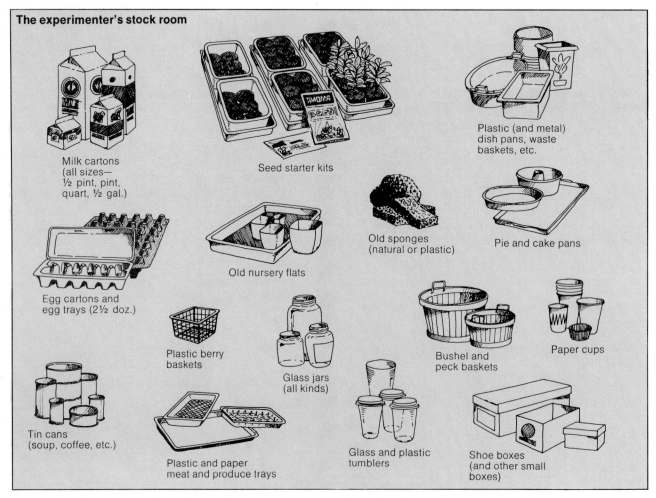

The experimenter's stock room

Milk cartons (all sizes— ½ pint, pint, quart, ½ gal.)

Seed starter kits

Plastic (and metal) dish pans, waste baskets, etc.

Egg cartons and egg trays (2½ doz.)

Old nursery flats

Old sponges (natural or plastic)

Pie and cake pans

Plastic berry baskets

Glass jars (all kinds)

Bushel and peck baskets

Paper cups

Tin cans (soup, coffee, etc.)

Plastic and paper meat and produce trays

Glass and plastic tumblers

Shoe boxes (and other small boxes)

The wonder of seeds

We think that, of all the seeds, beans give the most dramatic performance. The variation in shape and coloring when you gather the white and black and mottled seeds—lima, pinto, scarlet runner, horticultural, kidney, wrens egg and navy—is a visual wonder. But with them you can show that a seed is a dormant plant. It's alive. Built into it is a complete plant with a predetermined plan for growth—for roots, stems, leaves, flowers and fruits.

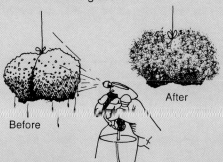

Pint jar
Blotter
Seeds
Water level
Plastic glass

Seedview jar and blotter. Use a pint jar and a 4 by 8 inch blotter. Fill jar with water to saturate blotter. Pour out all but 1 inch of water. Blotter will stick to the glass. Place seeds between blotter and jar. Add water when it goes below the 1 inch level. Place the jar in a warm dark place.

Seed view glass and paper towels. Line water glass or jar with 2 or 3 thicknesses of paper toweling. Put about 1 inch of water in the bottom of the glass and watch the paper soak up the water. Then place seeds between the moist paper and the glass.

To make sure that the paper towel remains firmly against the glass, stuff crumpled wet paper towels into the center of the glass.

Before   After

A growing sponge.
Wet a big sponge and squeeze out most of the moisture. Sprinkle it with annual rye, clover, cress or mustard seeds. Tie a string to the sponge and hang it in a sunny window. If you keep the sponge moist, the seeds will sprout and cover the sponge with green.

Germinating seeds are strong. Fill a small bottle or plastic vial with seed (peas or beans). Fill the bottle with water. Stopper the bottle with a cork or piece of plastic held tight by a rubber band. Wait about 6 to 8 hours for the swelling seeds to pop off the cork or lift up the plastic cover. Water moves into the seed cells through the seed walls. This swells the seed and puts pressure on the container. This principle was used to stretch a tight pair of leather shoes years ago.

Water   Tight cap

Patriotic celery. Use stalks of celery with leaves turning yellow. Place one in clear water, one in red ink or food color solution, and one in blue; leave in bright sunshine for a few hours. You should note some change in the leaves. A cut across a piece of celery left in solution should reveal that celery "strings" are really conducting tissue. Repeat your first experiment but use one stalk of celery split three ways and straddling all three solutions. What do you see?

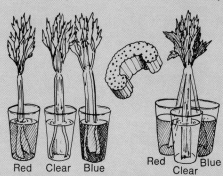

Red   Clear   Blue   Red   Clear   Blue

From generation to generation

The carrot, the avocado seed, sweet potato and pineapple have given their magic to the windowsill for children of all ages for hundreds of years.

Avocado.
Suspend an avocado seed in a jar of water with toothpicks. A couple of months after it sprouts you can transplant it to a pot. In a year or so it may look like this one.

Sweet potato.
Suspend a sweet potato in a shallow dish of water—it will root and become a quite spectacular, though temporary, houseplant. The shoots formed for decorative purposes can be used to start plants for the vegetable garden. Pinch off the shoots and plant them in peat pots. When they are 6-8 inches tall they are ready to be set out in the garden.

Carrot and pineapple tops.
An inch or two from the top of a carrot or pineapple spring to life and leaf out as if by magic when set in a shallow dish of water and placed in a sunny window. Try it also with beet and turnip tops. Will they grow too? What other vegetables can you make grow this way?

And they didn't miss the sights along the way

They watched roots grow...

We have always believed that the gardener blessed with a green thumb must have X-ray eyes. As he walks through the garden he seems to see into the soil. He knows how deep and wide the roots go--how much is "too much" and "too little" water. With a box designed to bring the below-ground action of plants into view the plant world takes on a new dimension.

According to teachers using the box the vegetable world comes alive in the eyes of the children. Roots and tops are seen as one. Roots develop rapidly showing a day-to-day change to sustain interest.

One way to make the box is diagrammed below. The dimensions are not critical. The box can be any length. We like to use a 2-foot long box. It's easy to move around but long enough to show off a dozen root vegetables. With two boxes you can compare growth in different soils or with different rates or methods of fertilizing.

How to build a root view box.

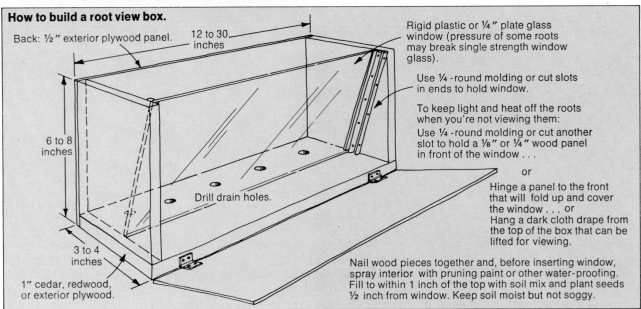

Back: ½" exterior plywood panel.

12 to 30 inches

Rigid plastic or ¼" plate glass window (pressure of some roots may break single strength window glass).

Use ¼-round molding or cut slots in ends to hold window.

To keep light and heat off the roots when you're not viewing them:
Use ¼-round molding or cut another slot to hold a ⅛" or ¼" wood panel in front of the window . . .

or

Hinge a panel to the front that will fold up and cover the window . . . or
Hang a dark cloth drape from the top of the box that can be lifted for viewing.

6 to 8 inches

Drill drain holes.

3 to 4 inches

1" cedar, redwood, or exterior plywood.

Nail wood pieces together and, before inserting window, spray interior with pruning paint or other water-proofing. Fill to within 1 inch of the top with soil mix and plant seeds ½ inch from window. Keep soil moist but not soggy.

You get fast underground action with radishes, and a lot of it before first leaves appear above ground. There's enough day to day change to make a root race a popular sporting event.

Milk carton root view boxes

Cut the top (for a vertical box) or the side (for a horizontal box) from a half-gallon milk carton. Cut out window area leaving about ½ inch of carton between corner and window. Cut glass to fit tightly into the corners of the carton. Waterproof glue or pruning paint may be used for a tighter seal.

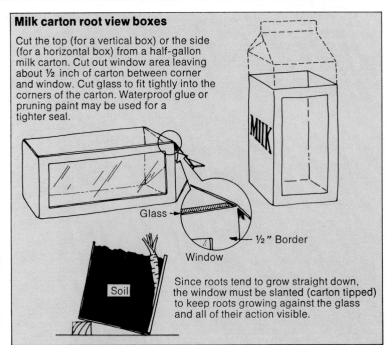

Glass

½" Border

Window

Soil

Since roots tend to grow straight down, the window must be slanted (carton tipped) to keep roots growing against the glass and all of their action visible.

...and seeds sprout

The child lives in a great big world, with a lot of things in it—things that crawl and things that swim; things that bark and things that cry meow; and things that *grow*.

If they become aware of things that grow, they become aware of a lot of other things. Like the sun and the wind, rain, and snow; like the changing seasons—the bursting buds of spring, the flowers of summer, the reds and yellows of the fall season. They begin to think of temperatures—the best air and soil temperatures for growing things. You become aware of the basic importance of the green world—all the bugs and animals and human beings depend upon it for food and fiber.

Don't miss the sights along the way from seed to plant and to seed again. Don't underestimate the power of plant growth to enrich the lives of children of all ages.

Above: the sprouting of onion seed. Seeds were planted at 4-day intervals to show the action from sprouting and the first small loop, to the extended seedling. The onion, like the bean, must pull the seed from the soil.

Below: the camera catches the critical moments in the birth of a bean when (top of panel) it is pulling the seed, now swollen and heavy with water, through the soil. Then the spring-action break out and the spreading of its pair of primary leaves.

95

Index